Volume the First

By Jane Austen

In Her Own Hand

INTRODUCTION BY
KATHRYN SUTHERLAND

Abbeville Press Publishers

NEW YORK LONDON

For the North American edition:
EDITOR: Joan Strasbaugh
DESIGN AND TYPESETTING: Ada Rodriguez
PRODUCTION MANAGER: Louise Kurtz

First published in the United States of America in 2014 by Abbeville Press, 137 Varick Street,
New York, NY 10013

First published in the United Kingdom in 2013 by the Bodleian Library, Broad Street, Oxford OX1 3BG

First edition
10 9 8 7 6 5 4 3 2 1

Library of Congress Cataloging-in-Publication Data

Austen, Jane, 1775–1817.
 [Works. Selections]
 Volume the first by Jane Austen : in her own hand / Jane Austen ; introduction by Kathryn
Sutherland. —First edition.
     pages cm. —(Jane Austen: in her own hand ; 1)
 Summary: "Volume the First is the first of three notebooks written by Jane Austen between the ages
of 11 and 12 and her late teens. Volume the First includes 13 stories and one poem, all written in her
own hand. An introduction by Kathryn Sutherland and transcription are included"—Provided by
publisher.
 ISBN 978-0-7892-1172-9 (hardback)
 1. Austen, Jane, 1775-1817—Manuscripts—Facsimiles. 2. Manuscripts, English—Facsimiles. I. Title.
II. Title: In her own hand.
 PR4032 2014
 828'.709—dc23
                    2014016066

For bulk and premium sales and for text adoption procedures, write to Customer Service Manager,
Abbeville Press, 137 Varick Street, New York, NY 10013, or call 1-800-ARTBOOK.

Visit Abbeville Press online at www.abbeville.com.

CONTENTS

A WRITER'S APPRENTICESHIP

Jane Austen grew up in a family of talented amateur writers who were also avid novel readers. Between 1811 and 1817, in a remarkable burst of creativity during her thirties, she completed six novels, *Sense and Sensibility, Pride and Prejudice, Mansfield Park, Emma, Northanger Abbey* and *Persuasion,* works which have carried her reputation throughout the world. But she was writing short sketches (fiction, drama and poetry) from as early as 1786 or 1787, aged 11 or 12, around the time she left the Abbey House School in Reading. Many, though not all, survive, as copies inscribed into three notebooks, which she confidently titled across their front boards "Volume the First," "Volume the Second" and "Volume the Third," in conscious imitation of the publishing format of a contemporary novel.[1] Running through these pieces is a pronounced thread of comment on and exuberant misreading of the fiction of her day, showing how thoroughly and how early the activity of critical reading informed her character as a writer. Jane Austen's first writings are comic imitations or parodies of popular novels; and they reveal that she was by her early teens familiar with a range of eighteenth-century English fiction. As she remarked years later, discussing the establishment of a local subscription library, in one of her earliest surviving letters:

> As an inducement to subscribe Mrs Martin tells us that her Collection is not to consist only of Novels, but of every kind of Literature &c &c—She might have spared this pretension to *our* family, who are great Novel-readers & not ashamed of being so;—but it was necessary I suppose to the self-consequence of half her Subscribers.[2]

In an age when writing for children was itself in infancy, the young Jane Austen was undoubtedly a precocious reader, but she was no snob: she devoured junk and high-end literature alike. We know she read modern classics like the multi-volume novels of Samuel Richardson (*Sir Charles Grandison* was a special favorite) and the latest pulp fiction—extravagant and improbable tales of gothic terror and sentimental romances. Her childhood library contained Arnaud Berquin's *L'ami des enfans* in French, possibly the gift of her French-speaking cousin Eliza, and Oliver Goldsmith's schoolroom textbook *The History of England*; while the distinctive cadences of Johnson's *Rambler* essays are mimicked and distorted in several of her own early tales.[3] The satirical form of her early writings suggests she relished the works she poked fun at; it also suggests a desire to entertain and impress with her cleverness.

STEVENTON RECTORY A pencil drawing of the side view of Jane Austen's home in Hampshire, England, where she composed her juvenilia, by her niece, Anna Lefroy, 1820.

All three juvenile notebooks are confidential publications;[4] that is, they are semi-public manuscripts whose internal features reveal they were intended and crafted for circulation among family and friends. They are not the secret confessions of a teenage girl, entrusted to her private journal and for her eyes alone. Rather, they are stories to be shared and admired by a select audience, filled with allusions to family jokes and events; they are sociable texts, the products of protective and indulgent circumstances. All three notebooks exhibit evidence of heavy wear, suggesting frequent rereading and family performance that can be securely dated before their acquisition by the holding libraries, where access has been limited and narrowly supervised.

The reader who turns to *Volume the First* from the restrained society of the adult novels might find its contents surprising, even shocking. Jane Austen's earliest writings are violent, restless, anarchic and exuberantly expressionistic. Drunkenness, female brawling, sexual misdemeanor and murder run riot across their pages. In the second piece, "Jack & Alice," an irresistibly eligible young gentleman, Charles Adams of Pammydiddle, sets steel traps on his estate to snare women who pursue him. Alice Johnson, a young woman with a drink and a gambling problem, in love with Charles, when out walking with Lady Williams, a local widow, probably also in love with Charles, comes across Lucy, "a lovely young Woman," also in love with Charles, "lying apparently in great pain beneath a Citron-tree" (p. 46). Lucy's leg has been broken in a trap and Lady Williams proceeds to reset it on the spot, performing "the operation with great skill which was the more wonderfull on account of her having never performed such a one before." But not before she has invited Lucy to tell her life story:

> "You seem fair Nymph to be labouring under some misfortune which we shall be happy to releive if you will inform us what it is. Will you favour us with your Life & adventures?"
>
> "Willingly Ladies, if you will be so kind as to be seated." They took their places & she thus began. (p. 46)

This is bad writing that glories in being bad: with its prosy and repetitious plot, and its compression or total omission of vital details of character and event, "Jack & Alice" is a catalogue of commonplace conventions and clumsy narrative contrivance. The setting of Pammydiddle is a clue to how to read it: a nonsense place name, perhaps derived from "Pam" (the knave of clubs and also a card game) and "diddle," meaning "cheat."[5] In "Henry and Eliza," entered into the notebook a few pages later, Eliza is a resourceful orphan who steals from one benefactress, elopes to France with the intended son-in-law of another, is widowed, returns to England with her children only to be thrown in prison, where the children, reduced to starvation, bite off two of her fingers, before she escapes and is finally reunited with her original benefactor, who discovers that, after all, Eliza is her long-lost daughter, abandoned at birth because her husband had wanted a son. All this is accomplished at headlong speed in under sixteen pages.

In contrast to the emphasis on psychology and the slow revelation of motive that characterizes the mature novels, these mini-novels proceed at a hectic pace: they are all action. Characters too are constantly on the move (they are prodigious walkers), and the humor relies on regional jokes (mock-Welsh and Irish names like Pammydiddle and Kilhoobery) as well as a sound knowledge of the map of central London (Bond Street, Hampstead, Portland Place and Bloomsbury Square). They are the virtuoso display of a writer who knows how fiction works, through plotting and narrative pattern, well enough to imitate a bad writer following a hackneyed paradigm. There were plenty of models on the shelves of the circulating and subscription libraries the Austen family were known to frequent. Works like the extravagantly titled *Anna: or Memoirs of a Welch Heiress: interspersed with Anecdotes of a Nabob*, of which one contemporary reviewer wrote: "In some parts of it the incidents are scarcely within the verge of probability; and the language is generally incorrect," before adding that "We have seen many worse novels; more dull in their progress, and more pernicious in their tendency."[6] *Charles and Charlotte*, a novel in letters, whose tone is hard to judge (because it is so clumsily written), tackles the risky topic of adulterous love. Rambling and sensational, filled like "Jack & Alice" with inset stories, it ricochets from one bizarre adventure to the next, and is written throughout in a heightened emotional style. Charlotte to Charles:

> My trunk, you may, if you please, forward to my apartment, and my sister (who being ignorant of our real situation had better be still kept so) I would recommend you to send home to her mother in the country, where the news, neither of our separation nor its motive, may ever arrive.[7]

At the conclusion of Lucy's recital of her adventures, Lady Williams exclaims: "Oh! Cruel Charles to wound the hearts & legs of all the fair" (p. 55), employing the rhetorical device of syllepsis. The young Austen is so proud of its effect that she is unable to resist repeating the trick later in the same story: "her Heart had formerly suffered by his charms & her Leg by his trap" (pp. 66–7). Syllepsis (sometimes called zeugma) is a construction in which one word (usually a verb) is applied to two words (nouns) simultaneously in two different senses. The passage from *Charles and Charlotte* (quoted above) almost, but not quite, descends into syllepsis. When, as in "Jack & Alice," the words thus yoked create an awkward alliance of abstract and concrete terms ("hearts & legs"), the effect achieved is a punning ambiguity that makes its own critical comment on the lurching style of the models its satire devours. As a bonus, it also plays falsely with the weighty antithetically balanced sentences that are part of the stock-in-trade of late-eighteenth-century prose masters and moralists, most notably of Dr Johnson. Jane Austen's early writings are regularly and joyously sylleptic.

Syllepsis connects Austen's youthful sketches with a whole tradition of English nonsense or absurdity, from Charles Lamb and Dickens to Edward Lear, in which the world is turned upside down and different kinds of reality collide in a lunatic logic of their own. In "The beautifull Cassandra" the heroine falls in love with "an elegant Bonnet" (p. 116) and proceeds to elope with it. In "Jack & Alice" the one character we never meet is Jack,

the Hero of this Novel ... of whom I beleive I have scarcely ever had occasion to speak;
which may perhaps be partly oweing to his unfortunate propensity to Liquor, which so
compleatly deprived him of the use of those faculties Nature had endowed him with, that
he never did anything worth mentioning. (pp. 61–2)

Other pieces in *Volume the First*, like "The adventures of Mr Harley" and "Amelia
Webster," turn the conventions of writing on their head. Ridiculously short, almost non-
existent, the challenge seems to be to discover how spare or elliptical a tale can be while
still containing the elements necessary for comprehension.

Unlike the adult manuscript writings (the novella *Lady Susan* and the unfinished fictions *The Watsons* and *Sanditon*), which, under public pressure, Jane Austen's nephew
and first biographer James Edward Austen-Leigh released in 1871 in his *Memoir of
Jane Austen*, all three juvenile notebooks were suppressed until the twentieth century.
The single exception was the dramatic sketch "The Mystery" from *Volume the First*
(pp. 140–45), included by Austen-Leigh to give "a specimen of the kind of transitory
amusement which Jane was continually supplying to the family party."[8] So far as the
nineteenth-century reading public was concerned, the juvenile writings simply did not
exist. It was not until 1922 that an edition of the hitherto unknown *Volume the Second*
appeared under the title *Love & Freindship and Other Early Works*, with an important preface by the English critic and comic writer G. K. Chesterton. *Volume the First*
was published several years later in 1933, and *Volume the Third* as late as 1951. This
means that while Austen's reputation as an adult novelist was well established during
the nineteenth century, it was left to the later twentieth century to develop an apprecia-
tion of her juvenilia. Early editors and biographers (still either Austen family members
or instructed by them as to what they knew) seemed reluctant to jeopardize a reputation founded in realism and naturalism by exposing to view the zany and surreal fiction
of the juvenilia; and, with few exceptions, the view persisted.

Chesterton was one such exception. In his preface to *Love & Freindship*, he aligned
the experiments of a 14-year-old Austen with the alternative tradition of buffoonery:
"She was the very reverse of a starched or a starved spinster; she could have been a buf-
foon like the Wife of Bath if she chose," and placed her in a comic line stretching from
Rabelais to Dickens.[9] He was not privy to the contents of *Volume the First*, still secreted
away in private hands, but he sensed that the early writings might be an opportunity to
rediscover the satirical and rebarbative aspects of the major novels lost sight of in the
sanctifying enthusiasm of Janeite adoration. In 1922 his estimation of the juvenilia was
well ahead of its time; it was not until the feminist revaluation of the 1970s that it would
be fully appreciated.

After her death in 1817 the bulk of Jane Austen's surviving manuscript fiction was held
in a single collection under the stewardship of her sister Cassandra. When Cassandra died
in 1845 the manuscripts were dispersed among family members: surviving brothers and

nieces and nephews. *Volume the First* went to Charles Austen, Jane's youngest brother. A scrap of paper attached to the front board of the notebook displays, in Cassandra's hand, the annotation "For my Brother Charles. I think I recollect that a few of the trifles in this Vol: were written expressly for his amusement. C. E. A." It remained in Charles Austen's family, descending eventually to his granddaughters, who sold various Jane Austen manuscripts in the 1920s, though *Volume the First* does not appear listed among them.[10] There is some uncertainty surrounding its ownership when Robert Chapman, the distinguished Austen editor and secretary to the delegates at Oxford University Press, tracked it down in November 1932 and arranged its purchase by the Friends of the Bodleian, for £75. Correspondence in the Friends' archive makes clear that even at the time the purchase price was considered a remarkable bargain. How much of a bargain might be illustrated by the fact that another Austen manuscript, the fair copy novella *Lady Susan*, sold at Sotheby's, London, only months later, in June 1933, for £2,100. The sale was completed in January 1933, Chapman retaining the notebook for several months, during which time he transcribed and edited the contents for the Clarendon Press.

If critics were slow to discover the literary importance of the juvenile manuscripts, it was because they could not connect them to the adult writings. Their freakish humor was clearly not to Chapman's taste; but his discomfort also extended to the look of the manuscript page—its blotted and untidy appearance. His commitment to an idealizing view of Austen's prose led him to be suspicious of compositional uncertainty. For him the immature hand was witness to the imagination as unformed and un-disciplined. Yet to other eyes, the blots, deletions and erasures in *Volume the First* tell a different story; one we can trace from the neat crossings through in its early pages (p. 15) to explosive splutterings of the pen (p. 44) and working revisions (p. 58) in the middle portion, and on to the blacker obliteration in "The Three Sisters" (pp. 158 and 166), and hatched crossings through (p. 174). There is a serious point here: changes in erasure—deteriorating through the manuscript from neat substitutions to more complex and consequently messier revision—are clear indications of changes in the status of the notebook itself—from a fair copy repository of completed writings to a surface for drafting new pieces and revising old ones. *Volume the First* holds precious clues to how Jane Austen worked.

The text of *Volume the First* is not simply a fair copy of writings composed in draft on other paper long since destroyed. Rather, it exhibits signs of complication through revision and the entry of items over a considerable length of time. Many small revisions to the early sketches were made during the initial transcription, but others are later additions. The dedication of "Frederic & Elfrida," the first item, to Martha Lloyd is written in a hand more mature than that of the work itself and probably dates to several years later than the actual entry of the story. The insertion "muslin" before "Cloak" (p. iv) ties the dedicatee even more firmly to this tale since Rebecca, a character within it, is an expert on the differences between Indian and English muslins (p. 7). The ten changes to this first story are almost all of single words, but revisions to the late story "The Three Sisters" are more extensive, including the deletion of three passages of several lines each. In one of these revisions, possibly entered in a hand other than Austen's, Mary, the eldest sister, demands new jewels on her marriage, including "Pearls, Rubies, Emeralds, and Beads out of number." This seems sufficiently extravagant, but originally the passage had read "Pearls as large as those of the Princess Badroulbadour, in the 4th Volume of the Arabian Nights and Rubies, Emeralds, Toppazes, Sapphires, Amythists, Turkey stones, Agate, Beads, Bugles & Garnets" (p. 162).[11] Other revisions to "The Three Sisters" rein in comic exuberance and discover a more resonant arrangement of the elements of Austen's sentence that anticipates the moral and acoustic balance of her mature work.

Smaller revisions to earlier pieces can be equally indicative of a sharpening critical sense. For example, in "Jack & Alice" (pp. 24–5), "agreable" is altered to "pleasing" to avoid the repetition provided by "disagreable" two lines earlier; and "inconvenience" is altered to "feirceness" (note the spelling "ei", favored by Austen throughout her manuscripts) because over the page "inconvenient" has been used. By contrast, later in the same tale she courts repetition of the same words for comic effect: "when a person has too great a degree of red in their Complexion, it gives their face in my opinion, too much colour red a look" (p. 37). The circular logic of this skillful revision serves to underline the unmistakeable fact of Alice's drunkenness. Later, a more complex revision replaces a neutral remark by Lady Williams with one contributing more effectively to her characteristic flow of backhanded compliments: "I may be partial; indeed I beleive I am; yes I am very partial to her" becomes "I am very partial to her, and perhaps am blinded by my affection, to her real defects" (p. 58). Though we cannot date these revisions, they point to the continuing service provided by even the slightest of the early sketches as a means to refine style and narrative skills over time.

All three notebooks demonstrate habits of writing and quirks of style that persisted into Jane Austen's later works, but *Volume the First* makes special claims on our attention. Of the three, it has the least straightforward chronology and its generic mix of short fictions, playlets, verses and moral fragments is least restrained. Its contents are simply more miscellaneous than those of *Volume the Second* and *Volume the Third*. Jane Austen wrote into a ready-made bound blank stationer's notebook, with marbled boards and quarter leather binding, and, according to a final inscription, completed the transcription on "June 3d 1793." Each of the notebooks contains internal details that date some of its pieces. In *Volume the First*, "The adventures of Mr Harley" (p. 104) has a dedication to Jane's brother Frank ("Mr Francis Willm Austen"), who was midshipman on the *Perseverance* between December 1789 and November 1791; so the latest composition date for the piece would be when she was 15 years old. Other pieces with terminal dates are: "Jack & Alice" (also dedicated to Frank); "The beautifull Cassandra," mentioned in the dedication to "Kitty, or the Bower" in *Volume the Third*; and "Henry & Eliza," dedicated to her cousin "Miss Cooper," who married Thomas Williams in December 1792. Changes in handwriting too show a division between entries in the earlier part of the notebook, where the hand is rounder and more childish (the comic sketches from "Frederic & Elfrida" down to the playlet "The Mystery," all dateable to the late 1780s), and the more mature hand of "The Three Sisters" (pp. 146 ff.) and the three pieces dedicated to Jane Austen's baby niece Anna, which Austen dated "June 2^d 1793" (p. 173).

By contrast, items in *Volume the Second* can all be placed securely between June 13, 1790, and before June 1793 (the date of the final items in *Volume the First*). As for *Volume the Third*, Austen dated its contents page "May 6th 1792" and the dedication to its second and final item "August 1792." This suggests that the writing and copying of the contents of *Volume the Second* and *Volume the Third* can be inserted either before "The Three Sisters" or after "The Three Sisters" and certainly before the pieces dedicated to baby Anna, listed on the Contents leaf of *Volume the First* as "Detached peices" (pp. i–ii). *Volume the First* therefore contains both the earliest and the latest items collected within the three juvenile notebooks, representing a period of six years, from 1787 to 1793, from age 11 or 12 to age 18.[12]

This chronology gives *Volume the First* a special interest. Unlike the other two juvenile notebooks, *Volume the First* bears clear indications that Jane Austen outgrew the original purpose and design she set for it. Yet she returned to it on two distinct occasions—probably for reasons of economy. "Love and Freindship," a "novel in a series of Letters" (dated "June 13th 1790"), is the first item in *Volume the Second* and it represents something new. It is also far too long to fit the pages remaining in *Volume the First* after "The Mystery." But "The Three Sisters," perhaps written as a wedding present for Jane's brother Edward and Elizabeth Bridges in late 1791, more than a year later than "Love and Freindship," was not too long; so it finds a place, out of chronology, in *Volume the First*. "The Three Sisters," like "Love and Freindship," is a novel in letters whose subject, preparations for a wedding, is especially suited as a gift to Edward and Elizabeth, herself one of three sisters, all of whom would marry within months of each other. Not only is it written out in a notably more mature hand than the earlier entries in *Volume the First*, the story's tone, a mix of farce and a new realism (it deals with a girl's reluctance to marry an older man) represents a distinct development, while extensive revisions and its unfinished state suggest it may have been composed as it was set down. This seems like a different use for the notebook.

Different again is Austen's second return to *Volume the First*, to fill its final pages (pp. 173 ff.) with the short "Detached peices" dedicated to Anna Austen, her second niece. Postdating the completion of *Volume the Second* and *Third*, these pieces not only fill *Volume the First* to capacity,[13] they turn economy to some structural purpose by mirroring the slightly earlier deployment of the final pages of *Volume the Second* to record "Scraps," as she calls them, to her firstborn niece Fanny. "Detached peices" are not easily connected with the earlier entries in the notebook (their tone is harder to discern), but like the "Scraps" in *Volume the Second* they appear to hand over the notebook to the next generation: "trusting that you will in time be older, and that through the care of your excellent Parents, You will one day or another be able to read written hand." It is worth noting that Jane Austen followed up this instruction a few years later when in 1801 she gave the young Anna her own copy of Ann Murry's *Mentoria; or, the Young Ladies Instructor*, a popular conduct book for girls. The copy of the second edition (1780) has the 9-year-old Jane Austen's ownership inscription (dated June 1785).

Part of the plan in copying these mini-novels, dramas and verses into a notebook and inscribing the cover "Volume the First" was to create a joke about book-making. This is a mock book and the way items appear on the page is a major part of the book's meaning in the original circumstances for which it was made. Hence the significance of a facsimile edition: the reader needs to see how the young Austen laid out her page to appreciate fully her intentions. By a variety of devices she invites us into the textual space. She consciously mimics through calligraphy the conventions of book-making—in paratextual features such as table of contents, dedications, titles and chapter divisions, and in the use of printers' rules (see the beautiful swelled rule on p. 106)—to create something like, but ultimately very unlike, a printed book. Presentational detail is a means of drawing closer to the literary models she parodies by recycling their formal codes (rather like the training involved in creating a school magazine). An important visual expression of the work's generic virtuosity, it contributes to the book as a performance for a particular audience— one that will recognize and share the joke.

The prefatory dedications attached to every item but one ("Edgar and Emma") welcome this audience, refigured in overblown terms as beneficent patrons of the aspiring author. It is worth noting that the word "Author" is used thirteen times in *Volume the First,* far more frequently than anywhere else in Austen's usually modestly voiced works. Though we now read *Volume the First* for its insight into the early imagination of a great writer, we should not forget this other original readership: *Volume the First* permits the modern reader a glimpse into the workings of coterie writing and reception within a rural gentry family at play at the end of the eighteenth century.

The physical structure of the notebook contributed to the way the young Austen refashioned these burlesque sketches as she copied them into its pages. Young though she was when she began to write into it, she can be seen deploying space with some skill: she knows to set aside two leaves before she begins to copy her sketches. These will later house her dedication to Martha Lloyd and a Contents list, which in view of Martha's lavishly placed dedication may have been pushed onto what might otherwise have served as a flyleaf. Changes in handwriting make it clear that some decisions about how to deploy space in order to create the mock book had to be made in advance; others were made much later. Several of the short sketches have dedications squeezed in as an afterthought (p. 22, for example), distorting and disrupting the spacious proportions originally given over to the titles, and suggesting that this aspect of the book-making joke grew in importance as Austen adapted to her writing surface and to the status the book may have acquired among family and friends.

The dedications, all but one ("Frederic & Elfrida" is dedicated to her close friend Martha Lloyd) to family members, are compositions in their own right and spin fanciful but provocative connections between dedicatee and story: two stories inscribed to Austen's youngest brother Charles, "Sir William Mountague" and "Memoirs of Mr Clifford," were probably written and dedicated when he was no more than 9. Their exploits, mixing seduction, partridge shooting, murder, more seduction, a passion for fancy carriages and travel, take on a particular cast with knowledge of his age. The miniature drama "The Visit" is dedicated to her eldest brother James, ten years her senior, who from 1782 to 1789 staged amateur theatricals with Austen family members at Steventon, complete with verse prologues and epilogues of his own composing. It is even possible that "The Visit" was performed by the young Austens in 1789.[14] In this dedication she recommends her play "to your Protection & Patronage, tho' inferior to those celebrated Comedies called 'The school for Jealousy' & 'The travelled Man,'" in the hope that it will "afford some amusement to so respectable a Curate as yourself; which was the end in veiw when they ^it^ was first composed by your Humble Servant the Author" (p. 126). Is this a reference to lost comedies written by James or by Jane Austen herself? The original reading of "they" (corrected to "it") suggests the latter possibility.

The page-long dedication to "The beautifull Cassandra" (p. 115) is a literary composition in itself. By comparison, the "story" that follows is simply a list of chapter headings. "The beautifull Cassandra" is gloriously anarchic, in its adventures and its stripping bare the mechanism of picaresque plotting. In other words, book convention is used to turn convention inside out. The early pieces in *Volume the First*, from "Frederic & Elfrida" to "The Mystery," are more accurately described as paratextual than textual: elaborate titles, dedications, chapter headings, but with minimal content. Their creative energy is lodged and discharged in the imitation and parody of bookish devices. *Volume the First* shouts its rhetorical effects out loud, and we need to see how Jane Austen laid out her pages in order to understand the joke.

Jane Austen did not simply outgrow her juvenile notebooks. There is ample evidence that she never finally closed their pages. The first drafts of the novels that eventually emerged as *Sense and Sensibility*, *Pride and Prejudice* and *Northanger Abbey* cannot easily be separated in time from the late juvenilia. There is evidence too that she rediscovered the notebooks in company with a younger generation, her nieces and nephew, through whom they lived again as family entertainment. For the modern reader, they provide a dramatic counter to the disciplined project of psychological realism which her published writings would lead her to develop. It is not too fanciful to find a trace of the females of the juvenilia in Elinor Dashwood's need of a stiff drink to help her cope with sister Marianne's hysterics: "'Dear Ma'am,' replied Elinor ... 'I have just left Marianne in bed ... if you will give me leave, I will drink the wine myself'" (*Sense and Sensibility*, chapter 30); and in Elizabeth Bennet's unladylike energy, "crossing field after field at a quick pace, jumping over stiles and springing over puddles" (*Pride and Prejudice*, chapter 7); or to hear in Mr. Collins, who scarcely cares which Bennet girl he marries, an echo of Mr. Watts from "The Three Sisters," for whom "it is equally the same to me which I marry of the three" (p. 161); or to discover as late as *Sanditon,* the novel Austen was drafting in her final months, that Diana Parker, applying friction to Mrs. Sheldon's coachman's ankle "with my own hand" "for six Hours without Intermission" (chapter 5), has walked straight out of the pages of *Volume the First*.

This facsimile edition of *Volume the First* has been produced with care to match the size of the original notebook, the appearance of its paper and the brown-black color of the iron gall ink that Jane Austen used. There is one important difference between Jane Austen's page and those of the facsimile, where the margins surrounding the original pages at top, sides and bottom have been extended in reproduction by several millimeters. We must imagine how closely she wrote to the edges and how little space she actually left. The transcription following the manuscript is that of the great twentieth-century Austen scholar Robert W. Chapman. Chapman was the first to edit Jane Austen's manuscripts in full and his early editions now have classic status.

NOTES

1. *Volume the First*, the earliest of the three juvenile manuscript notebooks, is held in the Bodleian Library, University of Oxford, England, MS. Don. e. 7; *Volume the Second* and *Volume the Third* are now held in the British Library, London. Together they contain writings composed and copied out between the ages of 11 or 12 and 17, though with evidence of corrections made considerably later.

2. *Jane Austen's Letters*, ed. Deirdre Le Faye, 3rd ed. (Oxford, England: Oxford University Press, 1995), p. 26, December 18, 1798.

3. David Gilson, "Jane Austen's Books," *The Book Collector* 23 (1974): pp. 27–34.

4. For "confidential" manuscript publication, see Donald Reiman, *The Study of Modern Manuscripts: Public, Confidential, and Private* (Baltimore: Johns Hopkins University Press, 1993).

5. As noted in *Catharine and Other Writings*, ed. Margaret Anne Doody and Douglas Murray (Oxford, England: Oxford University Press, 1993), p. 291.

6. [Anna Maria Bennett], *Anna; or, Memoirs of a Welch Heiress: interspersed with Anecdotes of a Nabob*, 4 vols. (London: William Lane, 1785); *Critical Review* 59 (June 1785): p. 476, cited in *The English Novel 1770–1829: A Bibliographical Survey of Prose Fiction Published in the British Isles*, ed. Peter Garside and James Raven, 2 vols. (Oxford, England: Oxford University Press, 2000), p. 352.

7. [Samuel Jackson Pratt], *Charles and Charlotte*, 2 vols. (London: William Lane, 1777), vol. 1, p. 19.

8. James Edward Austen-Leigh, *A Memoir of Jane Austen* [1871], ed. Kathryn Sutherland (Oxford, England: Oxford University Press, 2002), p. 40. In 1871 Austen-Leigh published *Lady Susan* and *The Watsons* in full but only severely pruned extracts from *Sanditon*.

9. G. K. Chesterton, preface to *Love & Freindship and Other Early Works, now first printed from the original ms. by Jane Austen* (London: Chatto & Windus, 1922), pp. xiv–v.

10. For details of ownership see the head note to *Volume the First*, available at www.janeausten.ac.uk, the Digital Edition of Jane Austen's Fiction Manuscripts, ed. Kathryn Sutherland (2010).

11. The revision could be in the hand of Austen's nephew James Edward Austen, who is known to have made changes to stories in *Volume the Third*.

12. Though the earliest pieces were composed when Austen was as young as 11 or 12, the hand suggests that they may not have been transcribed into the notebook before she was 14 or 15.

13. The final item in *Volume the First*, "Ode to Pity," is dedicated to "Miss Austen," probably Jane's sister Cassandra rather than Anna Austen. But this does not detract from the apparent use of the final pages to balance the use made of the end of *Volume the Second*.

14. This is the view of Paula Byrne, *Jane Austen and the Theatre* (London: Hambledon, 2002), p. 13.

Volume the First

15 aly

MS. Don. e. 7
= Arch. F. C. 32

Contents.

ii

To Miss Floyd

My dear Martha

     As a small testimony of the grati:tude I feel for your late generosity to me i finishing my muslin Cloak, I beg leave to offer ye this little production of your sincere Frein

            The Author

Frederic & Elfrida

a novel.—

Chapter the First.

The Uncle of Elfrida was the
Father of Frederic; in other words, they
~~were~~ first cousins by the Father's side.

Being both born in one day & both
~~b~~rought up at one school, it was not
~~wo~~nderfull that they should look on each
~~o~~ther with something more than bare po.
~~li~~teness. They loved with mutual sin:
~~ce~~rity but were both determined not to
~~tra~~nsgress the rules of Propriety by owning
~~the~~ir attachment, either to the object beloved, or
to any one else.

They were exceedingly handsome and so
much alike, that it was not every one
who knew them apart. — Nay even their
most intimate friends had nothing to
distinguish them by, but the shape of
the face; the colour of the Eye, the length
of the Nose & the difference of the com-
:plexion.

Elfrida had an intimate friend to
whom, being on a visit to an Aunt, she
wrote the following Letter.

To Miss Drummond

"Dear Charlotte"

    "I should be obliged to you, if you
"would buy me, during your stay with
"Mrs Williamson, a new & fashionable
"Bonnet, to suit the complexion of your
                                "E. Falknor."

Charlotte, whose character was a willingness to oblige every one; when she returned to the Country, brought her Freind the wished-for Bonnet, & so ended this little adventure, much to the satisfaction of all parties.

On her return to Crankhumdunberry (of which sweet village her father was Rector) Charlotte was received with the greatest Joy by Frederic & Elfrida, who, after pressing her alternately to their Bosoms, proposed to her to take a walk in a Grove of Poplars which led from the Parsonage to a verdant lawn enamelled with a variety of variegated flowers & watered by a purling Stream, brought from the Valley of Tempé by a passage under ground.

41

In this Grove they had scarcely re-
:mained above 9 hours, when they w
suddenly agreably surprized by hearin
a most delightfull voice warble the
following stanza.

Song.

That Damon was in love with me
    I once thought & beleiv'd
But now that he is not I see,
I fear I was deceiv'd.
_____

No sooner were the lines finis
than they beheld by a turning in
Grove 2 elegant young women lean
on each other's arm, who immedia
on perceiving them, took a different
path & disappeared from their sight

Chapter the Second.

As Elfrida & her companions, had seen enough of them to know that they were neither the 2 Miss Greens, nor Mrs Jackson & her Daughter, they could not help expressing their surprise at their appearance; till at length recollecting, that a new family had lately taken a House not far from the Grove, they hastened home, determined to lose no time in forming an ac: quaintance with 2 such amiable & worthy Girls, of which family they probably imagined them to be a part.

Agreable to such a determination, they went that very evening to pay their respects to Mrs Fitzroy & her two Daughters.

On being shewn into an elegant dressing
room, ornamented with festoons of artificial
flowers, they were struck with the enga
Exterior & beautifull outside of Jezabind
the eldest of the young Ladies; but eer th
had been many minutes seated, the Wit
Charms which shone resplendant in the
conversation of the amiable Rebecca, en
:chanted them so much that they all wi
one accord jumped up & exclaimed.

"Lovely & too charming Fair one, notwith
:standing your forbidding Squint, your
greazy tresses & your swelling Back, who
are more frightfull than imaginatio
can paint or pen describe, I cannot
refrain from expresing my raptures
at the engaging Qualities of your Min

hich so amply atone for the Horror, with

ich your first appearance must ever

pire the unwary visitor."

"Your sentiments so nobly expressed on

different excellencies of Indian & English

slins, & the judicious preference you give

former, have excited in me an admira:

n of which I can alone give an adequate

a, by assuring you it is nearly equal

what I feel for myself."

Then making a profound Curtesy

the amiable & abashed Rebecca, they

t the room & hurried home.

rom this period, the intimacy between

Families of Fitzroy, Drummond, and

lknor, daily encreased till at length it

w to such a pitch, that they did not

ple to kick one another out of the window

on the slightest provocation.

During this happy state of Harmon
the eldest Miss Fitzroy ran off with the
Coachman & the amiable Rebecca was
asked in marriage by Captain Roger of B
:inghamshire.

Mrs. Fitzroy did not approve of the
match on account of the tender years of
the young couple, Rebecca being but 36
& Captain Roger little more than 63. To
remedy this objection, it was agreed th
they should wait a little while till the
were a good deal older.

Chapter the third.

For the mean time the parents of Fre
:deric proposed to those of Elfrida, an uni
between them, which being accepted with

...leasure, the wedding cloathes were bought &
...thing remained to be settled but the naming
...the Day.

As to the lovely Charlotte, being im:
...ortuned with eagerness to pay another visit
...her Aunt, she determined to accept the
...itation & in consequence of it walked to
...r Fitzroys to take leave of the amiable Re:
...cca, whom she found surrounded by Patches
...wder, Pomatum & Paint with which she
...s vainly endeavouring to remedy the na:
...tural plainness of her face.

"I am come my amiable Rebecca, to
...ke my leave of you for the fortnight I am
...tined to spend with my aunt. Beleive
...this separation is painfull to me,
...t it is as necessary as the labour which
...ow engages you."

10/

"Why to tell you the truth my Love, repe
Rebecca, I have lately taken it into my
head to think (perhaps with little reason
that my complexion is by no means e:
:qual to the rest of my face & have therefor
taken, as you see, to white & red paint wh
I would scorn to use on any other occasion.
I hate art."

Charlotte, who perfectly understood the mea
:ing of her freind' speech, was too goodtempe
& obliging to refuse her, what she knew sh
wished,—a compliment; & they parted the
best freinds in the world.

With a heavy heart & streaming eyes
did she ascend the lovely vehicle* which
bore her from her freinds & home; but
greived as she was, she little thought
in what a strange & different manne

+ a post chaise

he should would return to it.

On her entrance into the city of London
which was the place of Mrs Williamson's
[re]side, the postilion, whose stupidity was
[am]azing, declared & declared even without
[the] least shame or Compunction, that
[ha]ving never been informed he was totally
ignorant of what part of the Town, he
[wa]s to drive to.

Charlotte, whose nature we have before
[in]timated, was an earnest desire to oblige
[ever]y one, with the greatest Condescension
[&] good humour informed him that he was
[to] drive to Portland Place, which he accor:
:dingly did, & Charlotte soon found herself in
[the] arms of a fond aunt.

Scarcely were they seated as usual

in the most affectionate manner in one
chair, than the Door suddenly opened & an
aged gentleman with a sallow face & old [...]
Coat, partly by intention & partly thro' wea
: ness was at the feet of the lovely Charlo[tte]
declaring his attachment to her & beseec[hing]
her pity in the most moving manner.

Not being able to resolve to make [any]
one miserable, she consented to become
his wife; where upon the Gentleman left [the]
room & all was quiet.

Their quiet however continued but
a short time, for on a second opening
of the door a young & Handsome Gentlem[an]
with a new blue coat, entered & intreat[ed]
from the lovely Charlotte, permission [to]
pay to her, his addresses.

There was a something in the appearance
of the second Stranger, that influenced
Charlotte in his favour, to the full as much
as the appearance of the first: she could
not account for it, but so it was.

Having therefore agreable to that
the natural turn of her mind to make
every one happy, promised to become his
Wife the next morning, he took his leave
& the two Ladies sat down to supper on
a young Leveret, a brace of Partridges, a
Leash of Pheasants & a Dozen of Pigeons.

Chapter the Fourth

It was not till the next morning
that Charlotte recollected the double engagement she had entered into; but when
she did, the reflection of her past folly,

operated so strongly on her mind, that she
resolved to be guilty of a greater, & to
that end threw herself into a deep stre
which ran thro' her aunts pleasure
grounds in Portland Place.

She floated to Crankhumdunberry
where she was picked up & buried; the
following epitaph, composed by Frederic
Elfrida & Rebecca, was placed on her tomb

Epitaph

Here lies our freind who having promi
That unto two she would be marri—ed
Threw her sweet Body & her lovely fa
Into the stream that runs thro' Portland
(Plac

_____

These sweet lines, as pathetic

s beautifull were never read by any one
ho passed that way, without a shower
f tears, which if they should fail of
citing in you, Reader, your mind must
unworthy to peruse them.

Having performed the last sad office
their departed friend, Frederic & Elfrida
gether with Captain Roger & Rebecca
turned to Mrs Fitzroy's at whose feet
tey threw themselves with one accor
addressed her in the following Manner.

"Madam"

"When the sweet Captain Roger
~~first~~ addressed the amiable Rebecca,
u alone objected to their union on
count of the tender years of the
rties. That plea can be no more,

16)
seven days being now expired, toget
with the lovely Charlotte, since the Capt.
first spoke to you on the subject."

"Consent then Madam to their w
& as a reward, this smelling Bottle w.
I enclose in my right hand, shall be yo.
& yours forever; I never will claim i.
again. But if you refuse to join their
hands in 3 days time, this dagger
which I enclose in my left shall .
steeped in your hearts blood."

"Speak then Madam & decide their
fate & yours."

Such gentle & sweet persuasion
could not fail of having the desire
effect. The answer they received, was n.

"My dear young freinds"

"The arguments you have used
are too just & too eloquent to be withstood;
Rebecca in 3 days time, you shall be
united to the Captain."

This speech, than which nothing
could be more satisfactory, was received
with Joy by all; & peace being once
more restored on all sides, Captain Roger
intreated Rebecca to favour them with a
song, in compliance with which request
having first assured them that she had
a terrible cold, she sung as follows.

Song

When Corydon went to the fair
He bought a red ribbon for Bess,
with which she encircled her hair
& made herself look very fess.

Chapter the fifth

At the end of 3 days Captain Roger an
Rebecca were united and immediately after
the Ceremony set off in the stage Waggon for
the Captains seat in Buckinghamshire.

The parents of Elfrida, alltho' they
earnestly wished to see her married to Frede
before they died, yet knowing the delicate
frame of her mind could ill bear the leas
exertion & rightly judging that naming her
wedding day would be too great a one, foreb
to press her on the subject.

Weeks & Fortnights flew away with
:out gaining the least ground; the Cloathes
grew out of fashion & at length Capt: Roger
& his Lady arrived, to pay a visit to their
Mother & introduce to her their beautiful

daughter of eighteen.

Elfrida, who had found her former ac=
quaintance were growing too old & too ugly
be any longer agreable, was rejoiced to
ar of the arrival of so pretty a girl as
leanor with whom she determined to form
e strictest freindship.

But the Happiness she had expected
rom an acquaintance with Eleanor, she
on found was not to be received, for she had
ot only the mortification of finding her=
lf treated by her as little less than an
to woman, but had actually the horror
f perceiving a growing passion in the
bosom of Frederic for the Daughter of the
amiable Rebecca.

The instant she had the first
idea of such an attachment, she flew to

Frederic & in a manner truly heroick
spluttered out to him her intention of
being married the next Day.

To one in his predicament who pos=
:ed less personal Courage than Frederic was
master of, such a speech would have been
Death; but he not being the least terrifi
boldly replied,

"Dammé Elfrida you may be married to
:morrow but I wont."

This answer distressed her too
much for her delicate Constitution. She a
:cordingly fainted & was in such a hurry
to have a succession of fainting fits,
that she had scarcely patience enough to
recover from one before she fell into another

Tho', in any threatening Danger to his
Life or liberty, Frederic was as bold as brass
& in other respects his heart was as
soft as cotton & immediately on hearing of
the dangerous way Elfrida was in, he flew
to her & finding her better than he had
been taught to expect, was united to her
forever —.

Finis.

Jack & Alice

a novel.

Is respectfully inscribed to Francis William Austen
Esq.r Midshipman on board his Majesty's ship the Perseverance
by his obedient humble
Servant The Author

Chapter the first

M.r Johnson was once up on a time about
53; in a twelvemonth afterwards he was
54, which so much delighted him that he
was determined to celebrate his next
Birth day by giving a Masquerade to his
Children & Freinds. Accordingly on the
Day he attained his 55.th year tickets
were dispatched to all his Neighbours
to that purpose. His acquaintance inde
in that part of the World were not very
numerous as they consisted only of Lady

Williams, Mr & Mrs Jones, Charles Adams
the 3 Miss Simpsons, who composed
the neighbourhood of Pammydiddle &
formed the Masquerade.

Before I proceed to give an account
of the Evening, it will be proper to
describe to my reader, the persons and
of the party
Characters introduced to his acquaintance.

Mr & Mrs Jones' were both rather tall
very passionate, but were in other
respects, good tempered, well behaved Peo:
ple. Charles Adams was an amiable,
accomplished & bewitching young Man;
of so dazzling a Beauty that none
but Eagles could look him in the Face.

Miss Simpson was pleasing in
her person, in her Manners & in her Disposi:
: tion;

an unbounded ambition was her only
fault. Her second sister Sukey was Envious
Spitefull & Malicious. Her person was
short, fat & disagreable. Cecilia (the
youngest) was perfectly handsome but too
affected to be ~~agreeable~~ pleasing.

In Lady Williams every virtue
met. She was a widow with a handsome
Jointure & the remains of a very hand:
:some face. Tho' Benevolent & Candid, she
was Generous & sincere; Tho' Pious & Good,
she was Religious & amiable, & Tho' Ele:
:gant & Agreable, she was Polished &
Entertaining.

The Johnsons were
a family of Love, & though a little ad:
:dicted to the Bottle & the Dice, had many

ood Qualities.

Such was the party assembled in
the elegant Drawing Room of Johnson
Court, amongst which the pleasing figure
of a Sultana was the most remarkable
of the female Masks. Of the Males a
mask representing the Sun, was the
most universally admired. The Beams
that darted from his Eyes were like those
of that glorious Luminary, tho' infinitely
superior. So strong were they that no
one dared venture within half a mile
of them; he had therefore the best part
of the Room to himself, its size not amounting
to more than 3 quarters of a mile
in length & half a one in breadth. The
Gentleman at last finding the fierceness

of his beams to be very inconvenient
to the concourse ~~of masche~~ by obliging
them to croud together in one corner of
the room, half shut his eyes by which
means, the Company discovered him to
be Charles Adams in his plain green
Coat, without any mask at all.

When their astonishment was
a little subsided their attention was
attracted by 2 Domino's who advanced
in a horrible Passion; they were both
very tall, but seemed in other respec~~ts~~
to have many good qualities. "These
"said the witty Charles, these are Mr
"& Mrs Jones." and so indeed they were.

No one could imagine who was the
Sultana! Tile at length on her address

beautifull Flora who was reclining in studied attitude on a couch, with "Oh Cecilia, I wish I was really what I pre: nd to be", she was discovered by the ver failing genius of Charles Adams, be the elegant but ambitious Caroline impson, & the person to whom she drefsed herself, he rightly imagined to her lovely but affected sister Cecilia.

The Company now advanced to a aming Table where sat 3 Dominos (each in their hand ith a bottle by his side) deeply engaged; A a female in the character of Virtue with hasty footsteps from the shock: g scene, whilst a little fat woman nresenting Envy, sate alternately on the

281

foreheads of the 3 Gamesters. Charles Ada

was still as bright as ever; he soon disco:

:vered the party at play, to be the 3 John

:sons, Envy to be Suker, Simpson & Virtue

to be Lady Williams.

The Masks were then all remo

& the Company retired to another room, t

partake of an elegant & well managed Ente

:tainment, after which the Bottle bei

pretty briskly pushed about by the 3

Johnsons, the whole party, not exceptin

even Virtue were carried home, Dead Drun

Chapter the Second

For three months did the Masque:
ade afford ample subject for conversation
the inhabitants of Pammydiddle; but no
Caracter at it was so fully expatiated
as Charles Adams. The singularity of his
appearance, the beams which darted from
his eyes, the brightness of his Wit, & the
whole tout ensemble of his person had sub:
dued the hearts of so many of the young
Ladies, that of the six present at the
Masquerade but five had returned uncap:
tivated. Alice Johnson was the unhappy
sixth whose heart had not been able to
withstand the power of his Charms. But as
may appear strange to my Readers,

that so much worth and Excellence as he

possessed should have conquered only hers,

it will be necessary to inform them the

the Miss Simpsons were defended from her

Power by Ambition, Envy, & Self-admiration.

Every wish of Caroline was centered

in a tiled Husband; whilst in Sukey such

superior excellence could only raise her Envy

not her Love, & Cecilia was too tenderly At-

:tacked to herself to be pleased with any

one besides. As for Lady Williams and

Mrs Jones, the former of them was too

sensible, to fall in love with one so

much her ~~inferior~~ Junior & the latter, tho' very

tall & very passionate was too fond of

her Husband to think of such a thing.

Yet in spite of every endeavour on
[the] part of Miss Johnson to discover any
[att]achment to her in him; the cold & in:
[d]ifferent heart of Charles Adams still to
[al]l appearance, preserved its native free:
[d]om; polite to all. but partial to none,
[he] still remained the lovely, the lively,
[&] insensible Charles Adams.

One evening, Alice finding herself
[so]mewhat heated by wine (no very un:
[co]mmon case) determined to seek a
[re]lief for her disordered Head & Love sick
[hea]rt in the Conversation of the intelligent
[Lad]y Williams.

She found her Ladyship at home
[as] was in general the case, for she was
[not] fond of going out, & like the great

Sir Charles Grandison scorned to deny herse
when at Home, as she looked on that
fashionable method of shutting out dis=
=agreable Visitors, as little less than
downright Bigamy.

In spite of the wine she had
been drinking, poor Alice was uncom=
=monly out of spirits; she could think
of nothing but Charles Adams, she could
talk of nothing but him, & in short spoke
                                        dis
so openly that Lady Williams soon per
covered the unreturned affection she bore him, which
excited her Pity & Compassion so strongly
that she addressed her in the following
Manner.

"I perceive but too plainly, my dear Al

hnson, that your Heart has not been

le to withstand the fascinating Charms

this young Man & I pity you sincerely.

it a first Love"?

is."

m still more grieved to hear that, I am

self a sad example of the Miseries, in

neral attendant on a first Love & I am"

termined for the future to avoid the like"

sfortune. I wish it may not be too"

te for you to do the same; if it is not"

ndeavour my dear Girl to secure your"

lf from so great a Danger. a second"

Attachment is seldom attended with

"any serious consequences; against that
"therefore I have nothing to say. Preserve
"yourself from a first Love & you need"
"not fear a second."

"You mentioned Madam something of
"your having yourself been a sufferer"
"by the misfortune you are so good as to
"wish me to avoid. Will you favour me
"with your Life & Adventures?"

"Willingly my Love."

Chapter the third

"My Father was a gentleman of considerable
fortune in Berkshire; myself & a few more
were only Children. I was but six years old when
I had the misfortune of losing my Mother &
being at that time young & Tender, my
Father instead of sending me to school, pro:
cured an able handed Governess to superin:
tend my Education at Home. My Brothers
were placed at Schools suitable to their
ages & my Sisters being all younger than
myself, remained still under the Care of
their Nurse."

"Miss Dickins was an excellent
Governess. She instructed me in the Paths
of Virtue; under her tuition I daily became

"more amiable, & ~~had not~~ might perhaps

"by this time have nearly attained perfec

"tion, had not my worthy Preceptoress been

"torn from my arms, ere I had attained my

"seventeenth year. I never shall forget her

"last words. "My dear Kitty she said. good

"nighttye". I never saw her afterwards"

"continued Lady Williams wiping her eyes,

"She eloped with the Butler the same nig.

year

  "I was invited the following ~~xmas~~

"by a distant relation of my Father's to

"spend the winter with her in town. Mr

"Watkins was a lady of Fashion, Family

fortune; (she was in general esteemed a
...tty Woman, but I never thought her
...ry handsome, for my part." She had too"
...gh a forehead, Her eyes were too small &"
...had too much colour."

...w can that be?" interrupted Miss Johnson
...ddening with anger; "Do you think that"
...one can have too much colour?"

...deed I do, & I'll tell you why I do. my dear"
...ce; when a person has too great a degree"
...ed in their Complexion, it gives their"
                           red a look." "
...ce in my opinion, too ~~much colour~~.

But can a face my Lady have too red"
look."?

"Certainly my dear Miss Johnson & I'll you

"why. When a face has too red a look it does

"not appear to so much advantage as it wou'

"were it paler."

"Pray Ma'am proceed in your story."

"Well, as I said before, I was invited by th

"Lady, to spend some weeks with her in to

"Many Gentlemen thought her Handsome"

"but in my opinion, Her forehead was too

"high, her eyes too small & she had too

"much colour."

"In that Madam as I said before your La

"ship must have been mistaken. Mrs"

"Watkins could not have too much colour

"since no one can have too much."

Excuse me my Love if I do not agree with
you in that particular. "Let me explain"
myself clearly; my idea# of the case is"
is#. When a Woman has too great a "
proportion of red in her Cheeks, she must"
have too much coloured."

But madam I deny that it is possible"
for any one to have too great a proportion"
of red in their Cheeks."
What my Love not if they have too "
much colour?"

      Miss Johnson was now out of
all patience, the more so perhaps as Lady
Williams still remained so inflexibly cool.
It must be remembered however that

her Ladyship had in one respect by far
the advantage of Alice; I mean in not be-
drunk, for heated with wine & raised by
Passion, she could have little command of
her Temper —.

The Dispute at length grew so
hot that on the part of Alice that,
"From words they she almost came to Blows
when Mr. Johnson luckily entered & with
some difficulty forced her away his Daught
from Lady Williams, Mrs Watkins & her
red cheeks.

Chapter the Fourth

My Readers may perhaps imagine that after such a fracas, no intimacy could longer subsist between the Johnsons and Lady Williams, but in that they are mistaken for her Ladyship was too sensible to be angry at a conduct which she could not help perceiving to be the natural consequence of inebriety & Alice had too sincere a respect for Lady Williams & too great a relish for her Claret, not to make every concession in her power.

A few days after their reconcilia-tion Lady Williams called on Miss Johnson to propose a walk in a Citron Grove which led from her Ladyship's pigstye to Charles Adams's Horsepond. Alice was

too sensible of Lady William's kindness in
proposing such a walk & too much pleased
with the prospect of seeing at the end of
it, a Horsepond of Charles's, not to accept
it with visible delight. They had not
proceeded far before she was roused from
the
⁁ reflection of the happiness she was
going to enjoy, by Lady Williams's thus
addressing her.

"I have as yet forborn my dear Alice
"to continue the narrative of my Life
"from an unwillingness of recalling to
"your Memory a scene which (since
"it reflects on you rather disgrace than

edit) had better be forgot than remem:
red."

Alice had already begun to colour
& was beginning to speak, when her
dyship perceiving her displeasure,
ntinued thus.

"I am afraid my dear Girl that I"
have offended you by what I have just"
id; I assure you I do not mean to"
istress you by a retrospection of what"
nnot now be helped; considering all"
tings I do not think you so much to"
lame as many People do; for when a"
rson is in Liquor, there is no answer:
ing"

"for what they may do;" ~~a~~

"~~situation is particularly offering you~~

"~~because her head is not strong enough~~

"~~to support intoxication~~"

"Madam, this is not to be borne; I insist

"My dear Girl don't vex yourself about

"the matter; I assure you I have entirely

"forgiven every thing respecting it; indee

"I was not angry at the time, as I sa ^{because}

"all along, you were nearly dead drunk

"I knew you could not help saying the

" strange things you did." But I see I di

"tress you; so I will change the subject &

sire it may never again be mentioned; re:
member it is all forgot— I will now "
pursue my story; but I must insist"
pon not giving you any description of "
rs Watkins; it would only be reviving old "
stories & as you never saw her, it can be"
othing to you, if her forehead was too high,"
r eyes were too small, or if she had too'
ch colour. "

gain! Lady Williams: this is too much—"

So provoked was poor Alice at this
newal of the old story, that I know
t what might have been the consequence
it, had not their attention been engaged

by another object. A lovely young Woman
lying apparently in great pain beneath
a Citron-tree, was an object too interesting
not to attract their notice. Forgetting
their own dispute they both with sim
:pathizing Tenderness advanced towards
& accosted her in these terms.

"You seem fair Nymph to be labouring
"under some misfortune which we shall
"be happy to releive if you will inform
"us what it is. Will you favour us with
"your Life & adventures?"

"Willingly Ladies, if you will be so kind as
"to be seated." They took their places & she
thus began.

Chapter the Fifth

"I am a native of North Wales & my
Father is one of the most capital Taylors
it. Having a numerous family, he was
~~sily~~ prevailed on by a sister of my Mother's
who ~~was~~ is a widow in good circumstances
keeps an alehouse in the next Village
ours, to let her take me & breed me up
2 her own expence. Accordingly I lived
with her for the last 8 years of my Life,
during which time ~~some~~ she provided me
with some of the first rate Masters, who

"taught me all the accomplishments requis

"for one of my sex and rank. Under their

"structions I learned Dancing, Music, Draw

"& various Languages, by which means I be:

":came more accomplished than any other

"Taylor's Daughter in Wales. Never was

"there a happier Creature than I was, till

"within the last half year — but I should "

"have told you before that the principal

"Estate in our Neighbourhood belongs to "

"Charles Adams, the owner of the brick "

"House, you see yonder. "

"Charles Adams! exclaimed the astonish

ice; "are you acquainted with Charles Adams?" —

"To my sorrow madam I am. He came"
about half a year ago to receive the rents"
of the Estate I have just mentioned. At that"
time I first saw him; as you seem ma'am"
acquainted with him, I need not describe"
to you how charming he is. I could not resist"
his attractions; —"

"Ah! who can," said alice with a deep sigh.

"My aunt being in terms of the"
greatest intimacy with his cook, deter-"
mined, at my request, to try whether"
she could discover, by means of her friend"
if there were any chance of his returning"

"my affection. For this purpose she went

"one evening to drink tea with Mrs Susan

"who in the course of Conversation mention'd

"the goodness of her Place & the Goodness"

"of her Master; upon which my aunt be-

": gan pumping her with so much dexte-

": rity that in a short time Susan owned,

"that she did not think her Master would

"ever marry," for (said she) he has often & often

"" declared to me that his wife, whoever

"" she might be, must possess, Youth, Beauty,

"" Birth, Wit, Merit, & Money. I have many"

"" a time (she continued) endeavoured to reason

"im out of his resolution & to convince him"

"f the improbability of his ever meeting"

"ith such a Lady; but my arguments have"

"d no effect & he continues as firm in his"

"etermination as ever." You may imagine"

"adies my distress on hearing this; for I"

"as fearfull that tho' possessed of Youth,"

"eauty, Wit & Merit, & tho' the probable"

"iress of my Aunts House & business,"

"might think me deficient in Rank,"

"in being so, unworthy of his hand."

"However I was determined to make"

"bold push & therefore wrote him a very"

"kind letter, offering him with great tender

":ness my hand & heart. To this I received an

"angry & peremptory refusal, but thinking

"it might be rather the effect of his mind

"than any ~~other desire~~ thing else, I pressed him aga

"on the subject. But he never answered a

"more of my letters & very soon afterwards

"left the Country. As soon as I heard of his

"departure I wrote to him here, informing

"him that I should ~~soon~~ shortly do myself the "

"honour of waiting on him at Pammy

": diddle, to which I received no answer

"therefore choosing to take silence for "

"consent, I left Wales, unknown to my

nt, & arrived here after a tedious journey "
is morning. On enquiring for his House "
was directed thro' this Wood, to the one "
u there see. With a heart elated by the "
pected happiness of beholding him. I "
tered it & had proceeded thus far in "
y progress thro' it, when I found myself "
dolenly seized by the leg & on examining "
e cause of it, found that I was caught "
n one of the steel traps so common "
gentleman's grounds. "

"Ah cried Lady Williams, how fortunate "
e are to meet with you; ~~&~~ since we might "
raise.
erhaps have shared the like misfortune "—

"It is indeed happy for you Ladies, that "

"I should have been a short time before

"you. I screamed as you ^{may} easily imagine till

"the woods resounded again & till one of

"the inhuman wretch's servants came

"to my assistance & released me from my

"dreadfull prison, but not before one of me

"legs was entirely broken."

Chapter the sixth

At this melancholy recital the fair eyes
Lady Williams, were suffused in tears &
[s]he could not help exclaiming,

"Oh! cruel Charles to wound the hearts &"
[le]gs of all the fair."

Lady Williams now interposed &
[obs]erved that the young Lady's leg ought to
[be] set without farther delay. after examining
[the] fracture therefore, she immediately began &
[pe]rformed the operation with great skill
[wh]ich was the more wonderfull on account
[of] her having never performed such a one be:
[for]e. Lucy, then arose from the ground &
[fin]ding that she could walk with the greater
[e]ase, accompanied them to Lady Williams'
[hou]se at her Ladyship's particular request.

The perfect form, the beautifull fa[ce]
& elegant manners of Lucy so won on
the affections of Alice that when they
parted, which was not till after Supper,
She afsured her that except her Fathe[r]
Brother, Uncles, Aunts, Cousins & other
relations, Lady Williams, Charles Adam[s]
& a few dozen more of particular frie[nds]
she loved her better than almost any
other person in the world.

Such a flattering afsurance of
her regard would justly have given m[uch]
pleasure to the object of it, had she not
plainly perceived that the amiable Al[ice]
had partaken too freely of Lady Williams's
claret. —

Her Ladyship (whose discernme[nt]

as great) read in the intelligent countenance

Lucy ^her thoughts on the subject & ~~when~~ ^as soon as

Miss Johnson had taken her leave, thus

addressed her.

"When you are more intimately"
acquainted with my Alice you will"
not be surprised, Lucy, to see the dear"
creature drink a little too much; for"
such things happen every day. She has"
many rare & charming qualities, but"
sobriety is not one of them. The whole"
family are indeed a sad drunken set."
I am sorry to say ~~too~~ that I never knew"
three such thorough Gamesters as they"
are, more particularly Alice. But she is"

"a charming girl. I fancy ~~that~~ not one of "

"the sweetest tempers in the world; to be "

"sure I have seen her in such passions! "

"However she is a sweet young Woman. "

"I am sure you'll like her. I scarcely know

"any one so amiable. — Oh! that you "

"could but have seen her the other ~~yesterday~~ Evening

"How she raved! & on such a trifle too! "

"She is indeed a most pleasing Girl! I sha

"always love her!"

        "She appears by your ladyship's ac:"

":count to have many good qualities," repli

Lucy. "Oh! a thousand," answered Lady "

"Williams; tho' ~~I may be partial, indeed~~ I am very partial to her, and

perhaps am blinded by my affection, to her

"~~I believe I am, yes I am very partial to~~

real defects."

Chapter the seventh

The next morning brought the three
[Mi]ss Simpsons to wait on Lady Williams,
[w]ho received them with the utmost po:
[li]teness & introduced to their acquaintance
[Lu]cy, with whom the eldest was so much
[plea]sed that at parting she declared her
[so]le ambition was to have her accompany
[the]m the next morning to Bath, whither
[the]y were going for some weeks.

"Lucy, said Lady Williams, is quite"
[at] her own disposal & if she chooses to"
[ac]cept so kind an invitation, I hope she"
[w]ill not hesitate, from any motives of"
[de]licacy on my account. I know not"
[in]deed how I shall ever be able to part"

"with her. She never was at Bath & I should
"think that it would be a most agreable
"jaunt to her. Speak my Love, continued
"she, turning to Lucy, what say you to
"accompanying these ladies? I shall be"
"miserable without you — 'twill be a mo.
"pleasant tour to you — I ⚹ hope you'll "
"go; if you do I am sure 'twill be the"
"Death of me — pray be persuaded" —

    Lucy begged leave to decline the
honour of accompanying them, with
many expressions of gratitude for the ex=
=tream politeness of Miss Simpson in
inviting her.

    Miss Simpson appeared much dis=

pointed by her refusal. Lady Williams
insisted on her going – declared that she
would never forgive her if she did not, and
that she should never survive it if she
did, & inshort used such persuasive
arguments that it was at length resolved
was to go. The Miss Simpsons called
her at ten o'clock the next morning &
Lady Williams had soon the satisfaction
of receiving from her young freind, the
pleasing intelligence of their safe arrival
at Bath.

It may now be proper to return
the Hero of this Novel, the brother
alice, of whom I beleive I have scarcely
ever had occasion to speak; which may
perhaps be partly oweing to his unfortu:
: nate

propensity to Liquor, which so compleatly
deprived him of the use of those faculti
nature had endowed him with, that he neve
did anything worth mentioning. His Deat
happened a short time after Lucy's depa
:sture & was the natural consequence
of this pernicious practice. By his de
:cease, his sister became the sole inheri
tress of a very large fortune, which as
it gave her fresh Hopes of rendering her
:self acceptable as a wife to Charles &
could not fail of being most pleasing
to her & as the effect was Joyfull the
Cause could scarcely be lamented.

Finding the violence of her at:
:tachment to him daily augment, sh

t length disclosed it to her Father &,

sired him to propose a union between

im to Charles. Her father consented & set

t one morning to open the affair to the

ung Man. Mr Johnson being a man of few

ds his part was soon performed & the

swer he received was as follows—

    "Sir, I may perhaps be expected to "

peared pleased at & gratefull for the offer "

have made me; but let me tell you that I "

sider it as an affront. I look upon my: "

f to be Sir a perfect Beauty — where "

uld you see a finer figure or a more "

arming face. Then, sir I imagine my

anners & address to be of the most po: "

shed kind; there is a certain elegance "

64

"a peculiar sweetness in them that I never
"saw equalled & cannot describe — Partiality
"aside, I am certainly more accomplished
"in every Language, every Science, every Art
"& every thing than any other person in
"Europe. My temper is even, my virtues
"innumerable, my self unparalleled. Since
"such Sir is my character, what do you
"mean by wishing me to marry your Daug.
"Let me give you a short sketch of yourself
"& of her. I look upon you Sir to be a very
"good sort of Man in the main; a drunken
"old Dog to be sure, but that's nothing to

our daughter sir, is neither sufficiently "

beautifull, sufficiently amiable, sufficiently "

witty, nor sufficiently rich for me. I "

pect nothing more in my wife than my "

if will find in me — Perfection. These "

are my sentiments & I honour myself "

having such. One freind I have & glory "

having but one. She is at present "

preparing my Dinner, but if you choose "

see her, she shall come & she will inform, "

n that these have ever been my senti: "

nts."

    Mr Johnson was satisfied; & expressing "

imself to be much obliged to ~~him~~ Mr Adams for the "

"characters he had favoured him with of him
:self & his Daughter, took his leave.

The unfortunate Alice on receiving
from her father the sad account of the
ill success his visit had been attended w.
could scarcely support the disappointme.
She flew to her Bottle & it was soon forg.t.

Chapter the eighth

While these affairs were transacting
at Pammydiddle, Lucy was conquering
ever Heart at Bath. A fortnight's reside.
there had nearly effaced from her remem
:brance the captivating form of Charles.
The recollection of what her Heart had

merly suffered by his charms & her leg by
s trap, enabled her to forget him with
terable Ease, which was what she deter:
                to, do;
ined; & for that purpose declicated five
nutes in every day to the employment
driving him from her remembrance.

    Her second Letter to Lady Williams
                                    having
tained the pleasing intelligence of her ^
omplished her undertaking to her entire
tisfaction; she mentioned in it also an
er of marriage she had received from the
he of —— an elderly Man of noble
tune whose ill health was the cheif
ducement of his Journey to Bath. "I am
istressed (she continued) to know whether"
mean to accept him or not. There are "

"a thousand advantages to be derived from

"a marriage with the Duke; for besides those

"more inferior ones of Rank & Fortune"

"it will procure me a home, which of all"

"other things is what I most desire. Your

"ladyship's kind wish of my always re:"

": maining with you, is noble & generous"

"but I cannot think of becoming so great

"a burden on one I so much love & esteem

That
"One should receive obligations only from
^

"those we despise, is a sentiment instill

mind
"into my by my worthy aunt, in my early

"years, & cannot in my opinion be too"

strictly adhered to. The excellent woman"
of whom I now speak, is I hear too much
incensed by my imprudent departure from
Wales, to receive me again — I most earnestly
wish to leave the Ladies I am now with.
Miss Simpson is indeed (setting aside"
ambition) very amiable, but her Sister"
envious & malevolent Sukey is too dis:
agreeable to live with. — I have reason to"
think that the admiration I have met with"
in the circles of the Great at this Place,"
has raised her Hatred & Envy; for often has"
she threatened, & sometimes endeavoured"
to cut my throat. — Your Ladyship will"

"therefore allow that I am not wrong in
"wishing to leave Bath, & in wishing to ha[ve]
"a home to receive me, when I do . I sha[ll]
"expect with impatience your advice concer[n]
": ing the Duke & am your most obliged
                                   &c &c — "Lucy."

        Lady Williams sent her, her opini[on]
on the subject in the following Manner.

        "Why do you hesitate my dearest"
"Lucy, a moment with respect to the Du[ke]
"I have enquired into his Character &
"find him to be an unprincipaled, illit[e]
": rate Man. Never shall my Lucy be unite[d]
"~~be united~~ to such a one! He has a poin[t]

ortune, which is every day increasing." "
ow nobly will you spend it; what credit "
ill you give him in the eyes of all; How "
much will he be respected on his wife's "
ccount! But why my dearest Lucy, why "
ill you not at once decide this affair by re: "
urning to me & never leaving me again? Altho' "
I admire your ~~the~~ noble sentiments with respect to "
bligations, yet, let me beg that they may not prevent ~~but I say If so If of If this~~
~~at to I sadly~~ your ^ making me happy. It will "
be sure be a great expence to me, to have "
me always with me — I shall not be able to "
pport it — but what is that in comparison "
ith the happiness I shall enjoy in your society "
will own one I know — you will not there: "
                                          :fore

72

"surely, withstand these arguments, or refuse

"return to yours most affectionately &c &

                                "E: Williams"

            Chapter the Ninth.

        What might have been the effect
of her Ladyship's advice, had it ever been
received by Lucy, is uncertain, as it reached
Bath a few Hours after she had breathed her
last. She fell a sacrifice to the Envy & Malice
of Sukey who jealous of her superior char
took her by poison from an admiring World
at the age of seventeen.

        Thus fell the amiable &
lovely Lucy whose Life had been marked
by no crime, and stained by no blemish

r imprudent departure from her aunt,
whose death was sincerely lamented
every one who knew her. Among the
ost afflicted of her freinds were Lady
illiams, Miss Johnson & the Duke; the
of whom had
first ~~having~~ a most sincere regard for
er, more particularly Alice, who had
ent a whole evening in her company &
ad never thought of her since. His grace's
fliction may likewise be easily accounted
r, since he lost one for whom he had ex:
evinced during the last ten days, a tender
ffection & sincere regard. He mourned her
with unshaken constancy for the next
fortnight at the end of which time, he
atified the ambition of Caroline Simpson

by raising her to the rank of a Dutchess.
Thus was she at length rendered compleat
happy in the gratification of her favourite
passion. Her sister the perfidious Sukey, was
likewise shortly after exalted in a manner
she truly deserved, & by her actions appeared
to have always desired. Her barbarous
Murder was discovered & in spite of every
interceeding freind she was speedily raised to
the Gallows. The beautifull but affected
Cecilia was too sensible of her own supe-
-rior charms, not to imagine that if Caro-
-line could engage a Duke, she might
without censure aspire to the affection
of some Prince — & knowing that those
of her native Country were cheifly engag

he left England. & I have since heard is the at present
favourite Sultana of the Great Mogul—.

In the mean time the inhabitants of
mmydiddle were in a state of the greatest
astonishment and wonder, a report being
circulated of the intended marriage of Charles
Adams. The Lady's name was still a secret.
Mrs Jones imagined it to be, Miss Johnson;
& she knew better; all her fears were
centered in his Cook, when to the astonishment of every one, he was publicly united
to Lady Williams.—

Finis

Edgar and Emma

a tale.

Chapter the first.

"I cannot imagine," said Sir Godfrey to his Lady, "why we continue in such deplorable "Lodgings as these, in a paltry Market-town, "while we have 3 good Houses of our own "situated in some of the finest parts of En- "gland, & perfectly ready to receive us!"

"I'm sure Sir Godfrey," replied Lady Marlow, "it has been much against my inclina-

that we have staid here so long; or why we
indeed, has been
should ever have come at all is to me a wonder
none of our Houses have been in the least
want of repair."

"Nay my dear", answered Sir Godfrey," you
are the last person who ought to be displeased
with what was always meant as a compli:
ment to you; for you cannot but be sensible
of the very great inconvenience your Daughters
& I have been put to, during the 2 years
we have remained crowded in these Lodgings
in order to give you pleasure."

"My dear," replied Lady Marlow, "How can
you stand & tell such lies, when you very well
know that it was merely to oblige the Girls

"& you, that I left a most commodious House

"situated in a most delightfull Country &

"surrounded by a most agreable Neighbour:

":hood, to live 2 years cramped up in Lodging

"three pair of Stairs high, in a smokey &

"unwholesome town, which has given me a

"continual fever & almost thrown me into a

"Consumption."

As, after a few more speeches on
both sides. they could not determine which
was the most to blame, they prudently laid
aside the debate, & having packed up their
Cloathes & paid their rent, they set out
the next morning with their 2 Daughters
for their seat in Sussex.

Sir Godfrey & Lady Marlow were indeed
very sensible people & tho' (as in this instance)
like many other sensible People, they some:
times did a foolish thing, yet in general
their actions were guided by Prudence &
regulated by discretion.

After a Journey of two days & a half
they arrived at Marlhurst in good health
& high spirits; so overjoyed were they all to
inhabit again a place, they had left with
mutual regret for two years, that they
desired the bells to be rung & distributed
nine pence among the Ringers.

Chapter the Second

The news of their arrival being quickly spread throughout the Country, brought them in a few Days visits of congratulation from every family in it.

Amongst the rest came the inhabi:tants of Willmot Lodge a beautifule Villa not far from Marlhurst. Mr Willmot was ~~younger~~ the representative of a very ancient Family & possessed besides his pa:.ternal Estate, a considerable share in a Lead mine & a ticket in the Lottery. His Lady was an agreable Woman. Their Children were too numerous to be particularly described; it is sufficient to say that

...neral they were virtuously inclined & not
...ven to any wicked ways. Their family being
... large to accompany them in every visit,
...y took nine with them alternately. When
...ir coach stopped at Sir Godfrey's door, the
...iss Marlow's Hearts throbbed in the eager
...xpectation of once more beholding a family
... dear to them. Emma the youngest (who was
...ore particularly interested in their arrival,
...ing attached to their eldest son) continued
...t her Dressing-room window in anxious
...pes of seeing young Edgar descend from
...e Carriage.

 Mr & Mrs Willmot with their three
...ldest Daughters first appeared — Emma
...as to ~~fear~~ tremble. Robert, Richard, Ralph,
...Rodolphus followed — Emma turned pale —

Their two youngest Girls were lifted from
the Coach – Emma sunk breathless on a
Sopha. A footman came to announce to
her the arrival of Company; her heart
was too full to contain its afflictions.
A confidante was necessary – In Thomas
she hoped to experience a faithfull one –
for one she must have & Thomas was
the only one at hand. To him she unbos=
herself without restraint & after owni=
her passion for young Willmot, requeste
his advice in what manner she should
conduct herself in the melancholy
Disappointment under which she la:
:boured.

Thomas, who would gladly have

en excused from listening to her complaint,

ged leave to decline giving any advice

                              much
cerning it, which ~~must~~ against her

ill, she was obliged to comply with.

Having dispatched him therefore with

any injunctions of secrecy, she descended

ith a heavy heart into the Parlour, where

e found the good Party seated in a social

anner round a blazing fire.

Chapter the third

Emma had continued in the Parlour

me time before she could summon up

fficient courage to ask Mrs Willmot

ter the rest of her family; & when she did,

                    faltering a   voice
was in so low, so ~~faltering~~

that no one knew she spoke. Dejected by
the ill success of her first attempt she ma
no other, till on Mrs Willmots desiring
one of the little girls to ring the bell for
their Carriage, she stepped across the room
& seizing the string said in a resolute
manner.

"Mrs Willmot, you do not stir"
"from this House till & you let me know
"how all the rest of your family do, part
":cularly your eldest son."

They were all greatly surprised
by such an unexpected address & the mos
so, on account of the manner in which it
was spoken; but Emma, who would not be

...gain disappointed, requesting an answer, Mrs

...illmot made the following eloquent oration.

"Our children are all ~~extremely~~ well but

At present most of them from home. Amy"

...s with my sister Clayton. Sam at Eton."

...ward with his Uncle John. Tom & Will at"

...inchester. Kitty at Queen's Square. Ned with"

...is Grandmother. Hetty & Patty in a convent"

...t Brussells. Edgar at college, Peter at"

...urse, & all the rest (except the nine here)"

..."home."

It was with difficulty that Emma

...ld refrain from tears on hearing of the

...sence of Edgar; she remained however

...erably composed till the Wilmot's were

gone when having no check to the overflow
of her greif, she gave free vent to them,
& retiring to her own room, continued in
tears the remainder of her life.

Finis.

Henry and Eliza

a novel.

umbly dedicated to Miss Cooper by her ob-
ient Humble Servant

The Author

As Sir George and Lady Harcourt
re superintending the Labours of their
ymakers, rewarding the industry of some
miles of approbation, & punishing the
eness of others, by a cudgel, they perceived
ng closely concealed beneath the thick
iage of a Haycock, a beautifull little Girl
 more than 3 months old.

Touched with the enchanting
aces of her face & delighted with the

infantine tho' sprightly answers she returned
to their many questions, they resolved to tak
her home &, having no children of their o
to educate her with care & cost.

Being good People themselves, t
first & principal care was to incite in
her a Love of Virtue & a Hatred of Vice, in
which they so well succeeded (Eliza hav
a natural turn that way herself) that
when She grew up, She was the delig
of all who knew her.

Beloved by Lady Harcourt, adore
by Sir George & admired by all the World,
she lived in a continued course of unin
:terrupted Happiness, till she had attain
her eighteenth year, when happening
one day to be detected in stealing a bas
:no

50 £, she was turned out of doors by her

human Benefactors. Such a transition to

who did not posess so noble & exalted

mind as Eliza, would have been Death, but

, happy in the conscious knowledge of

own Excellence, amused herself, as she

— beneath a tree with making & singing

following Lines.

Song.

————

Though misfortunes my footsteps may ever
                               attend

I hope I shall never have need of a
                               Freind

an innocent Heart I will ever preserve

nd will never from Virtue's dear boundaries
                               swerve.

————————

Having amused herself ~~with some~~

rs, with this song & her own pleasing

reflections, she arose & took the road to
M. a small market town of which p[.]
her most intimate friend kept the red L[.]

To this friend she immediately wen[t]
to whom having recounted her late mis:
:fortune, she communicated her wish of g[.]
into some family in the capacity of Hum[.]
Companion.

Mrs ~~Jones~~ Willsen, who was the most ami[.]
creature on earth, ~~had~~ was no sooner acquaint[ed]
with her Desire, than she sate down in
the Bar & wrote the following Letter to th[e]
Dutchess of F, the woman whom of all
others, she most Esteemed.

"To the Dutchess of F."

"Receive into your Family, at my

...uest a young woman of unexceptionable

...racter, who is so good as to choose your

...iety in preference to going to service."

...sten, & take her from the arms of your

"Sarah Wilson."

The Dutchess, whose freindship for

..s ~~Jones~~ Wilson would have carried her any lengths,

..s overjoyed at such an opportunity of

...iging her & ~~of expressing the love she~~ accordingly, sate out immediately

the

~~her~~ receipt of her letter for the ved

.., which she reached the same Evening.

...he Dutchess of F. was about 45 & a half,

..passions were strong, her freindships firm

...her Enmities, unconquerable. She was a

...dow & had only one Daughter who was

..the point of marriage with a young Man

of considerable fortune.

The Dutchess no sooner beheld a Heroine than throwing her arms around her neck, she declared herself so much pleased with her, that she was resolved they never more should part. Eliza was delighted with such a protestation of friendship, & after taking a most affecting leave of her dear Mrs Wilson accompanied her grace the next morning, to her seat in Surry.

With every expression of regard did the Dutchess introduce her to Lady Harriet, who was so much pleased with her appearance that she besought her, consider her as her sister, which Eliza with the greatest Condescension promised to do

Mr Cecil, the Lover of Lady Harriet, being often

with the family was often with Eliza. A mutual

...e took place & Cecil having declared his

...th, prevailed on Eliza to consent to a

...ate union, which was easy to be effected,

...Dutchess's chaplain being likewise

...y much in love with Eliza himself, would

...y were certain do anything to oblige her.

    The Dutchess & Lady Harriet being

...gaged one evening to an assembly, they

...k the opportunity of their absence & were

...ted by the enamoured Chaplain.

...When the Ladies returned, their amaze-

...ent was great at finding instead of Eliza

...e following Note.

Madam"

  "We are married & gone.

      Henry & Eliza Cecil."

as soon as she had read

Her grace ~~after having read it,~~ the letter,
which sufficiently explained the whole af
:fair, flew into the most violent passion &
after having spent an agreable half hour,
in calling them by all the shocking name
her rage could suggest to her, sent out ~~afte~~
after them 300 armed Men, with orders not
to return with out their Bodies, dead or alive; in
:tending that if they should be brought to he
in the latter condition to have them put to
Death in some torture like manner, after a
few years Confinement.

In the mean time Cecil & Eliza
continued their flight to the Continent, wh
they judged to be more secure than their
native Land, from the dreadfull effects of

e Dutchess's vengeance, which they had so

ch reason to apprehend.

In France they remained 3. years, during

ich time they became the parents of two

ys, & at the end of it Eliza became a widow

thout any thing to support either her or

children. They had lived since their

arriage at the rate of 12,000 £ a year, of

ich Mr Cecil's estate being rather less

n the twentieth part, they had been able

to we

save but a trifle, having lived to the

most extent of their Income.

Eliza, being perfectly conscious of

derangement in their affairs, immediately

her Husband's death set sail for England, in

an of War of 55 Guns, which they had

built in their more prosperous Days. But
no sooner had she stepped on Shore at Dou
with a Child in each hand, than she was
seized by the officers of the Dutchess, & con
:ducted by them to a snug little Newgate
of their Lady's, which she had erected for
the reception of her own private Prison

No sooner had Eliza entered her Dun
than the first thought which occurred to
her, was how to get out of it again.

She went to the door; but it was lock
She looked at the window; but it was bar
with iron; disappointed in both her expec
=tations, she despaired of effecting her Escap
when she fortunately perceived in a
Corner of her Cell, a small saw & a Ladd

...ropes. With the saw she instantly went

...work & in a few weeks had displaced every

...r but one to which she fastened the Ladder.

A difficulty then occurred which for

...retime, she knew not how to obviate. Her

...ildren were too small to get down the

...'der by themselves. nor would it be possible

...her to take them in her arms, when she

...-. At last she determined to fling down

...her Cloathes, of which she had a large

...ntity, & then having given them strict

...arge not to hurt themselves, threw her

...'dren after them. — She herself with ease

...cended by the Ladder, at the bottom of which

...had the pleasure of finding her little boys

...perfect Health & just asleep.

Her wardrobe she now saw a fatal necessity
selling, both for the preservation of her Childre[n]
& herself. With tears in her eyes, she parted w[ith]
these last reliques of her former Glory, & with
the money she got for them, bought others m[ore]
usefull, some playthings for her Boys and
a gold Watch for herself.

But—scarcely was she provide[d]
with the above-mentioned necessaries, than s[he]
began to find herself rather hungry, & had re[ason]
to think, by their biting off two of her finger[s]
that her Children were much in the same
situation.

To remedy these unavoidable mis
-fortunes, she determined to return to her
old friends, Sir George & Lady Harcourt, who

erosity she had so often experienced & hoped
experience as often again.

She had about 40 miles to travel before
could reach their hospitable Mansion, of
ich having walked 30 without stopping, she
nd herself at the Entrance of a Town, where
n in happier times, she had accompanied
George & Lady Harcourt to regale themselves
? a cold collation at one of the Inns.

The reflections that her adventures since
last time she had partaken of these happy
kettings, afforded her, occupied her mind, for
time, as she sate on the steps at the door
Gentleman's house. As soon as these reflec:
ins were ended, she arose & determined to
her Station at the very inn, she remembered
so much delight, from the Company of which,

as they went in & out, she hoped to receive so
Charitable Gratuity.

She had but just taken her post at the
Inn yard, before a Carriage drove out of it, & on
turning the Corner at which she was stationed,
stopped to give the Postilion an opportunity of admiring the beauty of the prospect. Eliza then
advanced to the carriage & was going to request
their Charity, when on fixing her Eyes on the
Lady, within it, she exclaimed,
"Lady Harcourt!"
To which the lady replied.
"Eliza!"
"Yes Madam it is the wretched Eliza herself.
Sir George, who was also in the Carriage, but too
much amazed to speak, was proceeding to demand
an explanation from Eliza of the Situation she
was then in, when lady Harcourt in transport

oy, exclaimed.

Sir George, Sir George, she is not only Eliza our
opted Daughter, but our real Child."

r real Child! What Lady Harcourt, do you mean?"
know you never even was with child. Explain"
self, I beseech you."

You must remember Sir George that when you
led for America, you left me breeding."

I do, I do, go on dear Polly."

Four months after you were gone, I was"
livered of this Girl, but dreading your just"
ntment at her not proving the Boy you"
hed. I took her to a Haycock & laid her down."

w weeks afterwards, you returned, & fortunately
me, made no enquiries on the subject. Satis:
within myself of the welfare of my Child, I

"soon forgot I had one, insomuch that when, we
"shortly after found them in the very Haycock, I
"had placed her, I had no more idea of her b
"my own, than you do, & nothing I will venture
                    had
"say would have recalled the circumstance to my
"membrance, but my thus accidentally hearing h
                    now strikes me as
"voice, which never before struck me with being
"the very counterpart of my own Child's."

        "The rational & convincing account you ha
"given of the whole affair, said Sir George, leave
"no doubt of her being our Daughter & as such
"I freely forgive the robbery she was guilty of."

        A mutual Reconciliation then took plac
& Eliza, ascending the Carriage with her two
Children returned to that home from which
had been absent nearly four years.

No sooner was she reinstated in her accustomed
[...] at Harcourt Hall, than she raised an
[...], with which she entirely demolished the
[Du]chess's newgate, snug as it was, and by that
gained the Blessings of thousands, & the
[...]ouse of her own Heart.

Finis

The adventures of

Mr Harley.

a short, but interesting Tale, is with all
imaginable Respect inscribed To Mr Francis William
Austen Midshipman on board his Majesty's Ship
Perseverance by his Obedient Servant The Author

Mr Harley was one of many Children
Destined by his father for the Church & by
his Mother for the Sea, desirous of pleasing
both, he prevailed on Sir John to obtain for him
a Chaplaincy on board a Man of War. He
accordingly, cut his Hair & sailed.

In half a year he returned & set off
in the Stage Coach for Hogsworth Green,
the seat of Emma. His fellow travellers
were, A man without a Hat, Another
with two, An old maid & a young Wife

This last appeared about 17 with fine dark
[eye]s & an elegant Shape; inshort Mr Harley
[soo]n found out, that she was his Emma &
[re]collected he had married her a few weeks
[befo]re he left England.

Finis

Sir William Mountague

an unfinished performance

is humbly dedicated to Charles John

Austen Esqre, by his most obedient humble

Servant

The Author.

————————

Sir William Mountague was

the son of Sir Henry Mountague, who was the

son of Sir John Mountague, a descendant of

Christopher Mountague, who was the nephew

of Sir Edward Mountague, whose ancestor was

Sir James Mountague a near relation of Sir

Mountague, who inherited the Title & Estate from

Frederic Mountague.

Sir William was about 17 when his Father
d. & left him a handsome fortune, an ancient
se & a Park well stocked with Deer. Sir William
not been long in the posession of his Estate
e he fell in Love with the 3 Miss Cliftons of
Kimbolton Park. These young Ladies were all
lly young, equally handsome, equally rich &
lly amiable — Sir William was equally in
with them all, & knowing not which to
fer, he left the Country & took Lodgings in a
ll Village near Dover.

In this retreat, to which he had retired
the hope of finding a Shelter from the Pangs
ve, he became enamoured ~~with~~ of a young Widow
ality, who came for change of air to the same
age, after the death of a Husband, whom she had
ys tenderly loved & now sincerely lamented.

108

Lady Percival was young, accomplished & lo

Sir William adored her & she consented to be

:come his Wife. Vehemently pressed by Sir W

to name the Day in which he might conduc

her to the Altar, she at length fixed on the

following Monday, which was the first of Sep

tember. Sir William was a Shot & could

not support the idea of losing such a Day,

for such a Cause. He begged her to delay

the Wedding a short time. Lady Percival wa

enraged & returned to London the next Morn

Sir William was sorry to lose her, he
as he knew, that he should   by
~~should~~ have been much more greived at u

Loss of the 1st of September, his Sorrow w

not without a mixture of Happiness, & his

Affliction was considerably lessened by his

Joy.
                                                        the
After staying at a Village a few wee

longer, he left it & went to a friend's Hous

Surry. Mr Brudenell was a sensible Man, &
a beautifull Neice with whom Sir William
fell in love. But Miss Arundel was cruel;
preferred a Mr Stanhope: Sir William shot
Stanhope; the lady had then no reason to
use him; she accepted him, & they were to
married on the 27.th of October. But on the
M. Sir William received a visit from Emma
nhope the sister of the unfortunate Victim
his rage. She begged some recompence, some
nement for the cruel Murder of her Brother.
William bade her name her price. She fixed
14. Sir William offered her himself &
tune. They went to London the next day &
there privately married. For a fortnight
William was compleatly happy, but
neing one day to see a charming young

110

Woman entering a Chariot in Brook Street, he
became again most violently in love. On
enquiring the name of this fair Unknown
he found that she was the Sister of his old
freind Lady Percival, at which he was m
rejoiced, as he hoped to have, by his acquain
=tance with her Ladyship, free access to My
Wentworth . . . .

Finis

To Charles John Austen Esqre

————————————

Sir,

Your generous patronage of the
unfinished tale, I have already taken the
liberty of dedicating to you, encourages
me to dedicate to you a second, as unfinish:
d as the first.

I am Sir with every expression
of regard for you & yr noble
Family; your most obed:
^t
U S — . .
The Author

Memoirs of Mr Clifford

an unfinished Tale —

Mr Clifford lived at Bath; & having
never seen London, set off one monday morn
determined to feast his eyes with a sight of the
great Metropolis. He travelled in his Coach & Fou
for he was a very rich young Man & kept a
great many Carriages of which I do not recolle
half. I can only remember that he had a Coac
a Chariot, a Chaise, a Landau, a Landaulet, a
Phaeton, a Gig, a Whiskey, an italian Chair, a
Buggy, a Curricle & a wheelbarrow. He had
likewise an amazing fine stud of Horses.
my knowledge he had six Greys, 4 Bays, a

...cks & a pony.

In his Coach & 4 Bays Mr Clifford satt-
ed about 5 o'clock on Monday morning
ye 1st of May. for London. He always travelled
remarkably expeditiously & contrived therefore
get to Devizes from Bath, which is no less
nineteen miles, the first Day. To be sure
did not get in till eleven at night & pretty
ht work it was as you may imagine.

However when he was once got to Devizes
was determined to comfort himself with
ood hot Supper and therefore ordered a
hole Egg to be boiled for him & his Servants.
e next morning he pursued his Journey
in the course of 3 days hard labour reached
rton, where he was siezed with a ~~violent~~ dangerous fever
onsequence of too violent Exercise.

Five months did our Hero remain in the celebrated City under the care of its no less cele: :brated Physician, who at length compleatly cured him of his troublesome Desease.

As Mr Clifford still continued very weak, his first Days Journey carried him only to Dean Gate, where he remained a few Days & found himself much benefited by the change of air.

In easy Stages he proceeded to Basingstoke one day Carrying him to Clarkengreen, the next to Worting, the 3.d to the bottom of Basingstoke Hill, & the fourth, to Mr Robinson's. . . . .

Finis

The beautifull Cassandra

a novel in twelve Chapters.

dedicated by permission to Miss Austen.
Dedication.

Madam

You are a Phoenix. Your taste is refined,
your sentiments are noble, & your Virtues
innumerable. Your Person is lovely, your
figure, elegant, & your Form, majestic. Your
manners are polished, your Conversation is
rational & your appearance singular.
If therefore the following Tale will
afford one moments amusement to
you, every wish will be gratified of
your most obedient
humble Servant
The Author

The beautifull Cassandra.

a novel, in twelve Chapters.

Chapter the first

Cassandra was the Daughter and the only Daughter of a celebrated Millener in Bond Street. Her father was of noble Birth, being the near relation of the Dutchess of —'s Butler.

Chapter the 2d

When Cassandra had attained her 16th year, she was lovely & amiable & chancing to fall in love with an elegant Bonnett, her Mother had just compleated bespoke by the Countess of —— she placed it on her gentle Head & walked from her Mothers shop to make her Fortune.

Chapter the 3d

The first person she met, was the Visc

— a young Man, no less celebrated for his Ac=
complishments & Virtues, than for his Elegance
Beauty. She curtseyed & walked on.

Chapter the 4th.

She then proceeded to a Pastry cooks where
devoured six ices, refused to pay for them,
knocked down the Pastry Cook & walked away.

Chapter the 5th.

She next ascended a Hackney Coach & ordered
to Hampstead, where she was no sooner arrived
than she ordered the Coachman to turn round
drive her back again.

Chapter the 6th

Being returned to the same spot of
same street she had sate out from, the
Coachman demanded his Pay.

Chapter the 7th

She searched her pockets over again & aga
but every search was unsuccessfull. No money
could she find. The man grew ~~impatient~~. She
placed her bonnet on his head & ran away.

promptory.

Chapter the 8th

Thro' many a street she then proceeded
& met in none the least Adventure till on
turning a Corner of Bloomsbury Square, she
met Maria.

Chapter the 9th

Cassandra started & Maria seemed sur
:prised; they trembled, blushed, turned pale &
passed each other in a mutual silence.

Chapter the 10th

Cassandra was next accosted by her

hind the Widow, who squeezing out her little
d thro' her lefs window, asked her how she did?
assandra curtsied & went on.

——— Chapter the 11th ———

a quarter of a mile brought her to her
ternal roof in Bond Street, from which she
d now been absent nearly 7 hours.

——— Chapter the 12th ———

She entered it & was prefsed to her Mo:
ther's bosom by that worthy Woman. Cassandra
iled & whispered to herself "This is a day
ll spent."

——— Finis. ———

Amelia Webster

an interesting & well written Tale

is dedicated by Permission
to
Mrs Austen
by
Her humble Servant

The Author.

Letter the first

　　　　To Miss Webster

My dear Amelia

　　　You will rejoice to hear of the return
my amiable Brother from abroad. He arrived
thursday, & never did I see a finer form,
re that of your sincere friend

　　　　　　　　　Matilda Hervey

Letter the 2

　　　　To A. Beverley Esqre

Dear Beverley

　　　I arrived here last thursday & met
with a hearty reception from my Father,
ther & Sisters. The latter are both fine.
ilo – particularly Maud, who I think would
it you as a Wife – well enough. What say you

122

to this? She will have two thousand Pound
& as much more as you can get. If you don
marry her you will mortally offend
George Hervey

Letter the 3.ᵈ

To Miss Hervey

Dear Maud

Beleive me I'm happy to hear of
your Brother's arrival. I have a thousand
things to tell you, but my paper will only
permit one to add that I am y.ʳ "affe.ᵗ" Frein
Amelia Webster

Letter the 4.ᵗʰ

To Miss S. Hervey

Dear Sally

I have found a very convenient

hollow oak to put our letters in: for you
ow we have long maintained a private
espondence. It is about a mile from my
se & seven from yours. You may perhaps
agine that I might have made choice
a tree which would have divided the Dis:
nce more equally — I was sensible of
s at the time, but as I considered that
walk would be of benefit to you in your
k & uncertain state of Health, I preferred
to one nearer your House, & am y.ᵐ faithfull
                          Benjamin Bar

tter the 5.ᵗʰ
              To Miss Hervey
ear Maud
        I write now to inform you that I
not stop at your house in my way to

Bath last Monday. — I have many things
besides;
to inform you of, but my Paper remind
one of concluding; & beleive me y.rs ever &.
                                    Amelia Webster.

Letter the 6.th
            To Miss Webster

Madam
                                    Saturd
            An humble Admirer now address
you — I saw you lovely Fair one as you
passed on Monday last, before our House
in your way to Bath. I saw you thro' a
telescope, & was so struck by your Char
that from that time to this I have
not tasted human food.
                        George Hervey.

Letter the 7.th
            To Jack

As I was this morning at Breakfast
a Newspaper was brought me; & in the list
marriages I read the following.

"George Hervey Esq.re to Miss Amelia Webster"

"Henry Beverley Esq.re to Miss Hervey"

&

Benjamin Bar Esq.re to Miss Sarah Hervey.

Yours, Tom.

Finis —

The Visit

a comedy in 2 acts

Dedication.

To the Revd James Austen.

Sir,
    The following Drama, which I humbly
recommend to your Protection & Patronage
tho' inferior to those celebrated Comedies
called "The School for Jealousy" & "The travelled
Man", will I hope afford some amuse-
:ment to so respectable a <u>Curate</u> as
yourself; which was the end in view
        it
when ~~they~~ was first composed by your
Humble Servant the Author.

Dramatis Personae

Sir Arthur Hampton

Lord Fitzgerald

Stanly

Willoughby, Sir Arthur's nephew.

Lady Hampton

Miss Fitzgerald

Sophy Hampton

Cloe Willoughby

The scenes are laid in
Lord Fitzgerald's House.

128

Act the First

Scene the first . a Parlour .

enter Lord Fitzgerald & Stanley

Stanly. Cousin your servant.

Fitzgerald. Stanly, good morning to you. I hope
you slept well last night.

Stanly. Remarkably well, I thank you.

Fitzgerald. I am afraid you found your Bed
too short. It was bought in my
grandmother's time, who was herself
a very short woman & made a point of
suiting all her Beds to her own length,
as she never wished to have any com=
=pany in the House, on account of

unfortunate impediment in her speech,
which she was sensible of being very
disagreable to her inmates.

nly. Make no more excuses dear Fitzgerald

tzgerald. I will not distress you by too
    much civility — I only beg you will
    consider yourself as much at home
as in your Father's house. Remember,
"The more free, the more Wellcome".

               (exit Fitzgerald)

nly. Amiable Youth!

  Your virtues could he imitate
How happy would be Stanly's fate!

              (exit Stanly.)

Scene the 2.^d

Stanly & Miss Fitzgerald, discovered.

———

Stanly. What Company is it you expect
to dine with you to Day, Cousin?

Miss F. Sir Arthur & Lady Hampton; their
Daughter, Nephew & Niece.

Stanly. Miss Hampton & her Cousin are both
Handsome, are they not?

Miss F. Miss Willoughby is extreamly so.
Miss Hampton is a fine Girl, but not
equal to her.

Stanly. Is not your Brother Attached to the
Latter?

Miss F. He admires her I know, but I beleive
nothing more. Indeed I have heard h

that she was the most beautifull, pleas=

=ing, & amiable Girl in the world, &

that of all others he should prefer her

for his Wife". But it never went farther ans

I'm certain.

only. And yet my Cousin never says

a thing he does not mean.

Is F. Never. From his Cradle he has ~~ever~~ always

been a strict adherent to Truth. ~~He~~

~~never told a lie but once, & that was~~

~~merely to oblige me. Indeed I may~~

~~truly say there never was in his~~

~~brother!~~

(Exeunt severally)

End of the First Act.

Act the Second

Scene the first, The Drawing Room

Chairs set round in a row. Lord Fitzg

Miss Fitzgerald & Stanly seated.

Enter a Servant.

Servant. Sir Arthur & Lady Hampton. s

Hampton, Mr & Miss Willoughby.

(exit Serv

Enter the Company.

Miss F. I hope I have the pleasure of

seeing your Ladyship well. Sir Arth

your servant. Yr Mr Willoughby.

Dear Sophy, Dear Cloe, ——

(They pay their Compliments

alternately.)

ls F. Pray be seated.

(They sit)

Bless me! there ought to be 8 Chairs
& there are but 6. However, if your
Ladyship will but take Sir Arthur
in your Lap, & Sophy, ~~take~~ my Brother
in hers, I believe we shall do pretty
well.

y H. Oh! with pleasure . . .

hy. I beg his Lordship would be seated.

ls F. I am really shocked at crowding
you in such a manner, but my
Grandmother (who bought all the
furniture of this room) as she had
never a very large Party, did not think
t necessary to buy more Chairs than
ere sufficient for her own family and

two of her particular freinds.

Sophy. I beg you will make no apologi
  Your Brother is very light.

Stanly, aside) What a cherub is Cloe!

Cloe, aside) What a seraph is Stanly!

   Enter a Servant.

Servant. Dinner is on table.

   They all rise.

Miss F. Lady Hampton, Miss Hampton
  Miss Willoughby.

Stanly hands Cloe, Lord Fitzgerald, So
Willoughby, Miss Fitzgerald, and Sir arth
Lady Hampton.

   (Exeunt.)

Scene the 2^d

The Dining Parlour.

...ss Fitzgerald at top. Lord Fitzgerald at
...ttom. Company ranged on each side.

Servants waiting.

... I shall trouble Mr Stanly for a
little of the, fried Cowheel & onion.

...nly. Oh Madam, there is a secret pleasure
in helping so amiable a Lady ——.

...y H. I assure you my Lord, Sir Arthur
never touches wine; but ~~however~~
Sophy will toss off a Bumper I am
...ure to oblige your Lordship.

...d F. Elder wine or Mead, Miss Hampton?

...hy. If it is equal to you Sir, I should
                                    a toast and
prefer some warm ale with ~~#~~ nutmeg.

Lord F. Two glasses of warmed ale with a
and nutmeg.

Miss F. I am afraid Mr Willoughby, you
take no care of yourself. I fear
don't meet with any thing to your
liking.

Willoughby. Oh! Madam, I can want for
nothing while there are red herring
on table.

Lord F. Sir arthur taste that Tripe. I th
you will not find it amiss.

Lady H. Sir arthur never eats Tripe; 'tis a
savoury for ~~him~~ him, you know my Lo

Miss F. Take away the Liver & Crow & brin
in the Suet pudding.
            (a short Pause.)

Miss F. Sir arthur shant I send yo

bit of pudding?

Lady H. Sir Arthur never eats suet pudding

  Ma'am. It is too high a Dish for him.

Miss F. Will no one allow me the honour

   of helping them? Then John take

away the Pudding, & bring the Wine.

vants take away the things and bring

  the Bottles & Glasses.)

d F. I wish we had any Desert to

offer you.. But my Grandmother in

her Life time, destroyed the Hot house

in order to build a receptacle for the

Turkies with it's materials; & we

have never been able to raise another

tolerable one.

y H. I beg you will make no apologies

           my Lord.

Willoughby. Come Girls, let us circulate
    the Bottle.

Sophy. A very good motion Cousin; & I
    will second it with all my Heart
    Stanly you dont drink.

Stanly. Madam, I am drinking draughts
    of Love from Clve's eyes.

Sophy. That's poor nourishment truly
    Come, drink to her better acquaintance

(Miss Fitzgerald goes to a Closet & brings
                 a bottle)

Miss F. This, Ladies & Gentlemen is some
    of my dear Grandmother's own ma:
    :nufacture. She excelled in Gooseberry
    Pray taste it Lady Hampton?

Lady H. How refreshing it is!

ifs F. I should think with your Ladyship's
permission, that Sir Arthur might
taste a little of it.

ly H. Not for worlds. Sir Arthur never
drinks any thing so high.

d F. And now my amiable Sophia
condescend to marry me.

(takes her hand & leads her to the front)

nly. Oh! Cloe could I but hope you
would make me blessed ——

e. I will.

(They advance.)

ifs F. Since you Willoughby are the
only one left, I cannot refuse your
earnest solicitations — There is my
hand. —

ady H. And may you all be Happy!

Finis.

The Mystery

an unfinished Comedy.

Dedication

To the Rev: George Austen

Sir

    I humbly solicit your Patronage to the following Comedy, which tho' an unfinished one, is I flatter myself as <u>complete</u> a <u>Mystery</u> as any of its kind.

        I am Sir your most Humble Servant

          The Author

The Mystery

a Comedy —

Dramatis Personae

Men.

Colonel Elliott

Sir Edward Spangle

Old Humbug

Young Humbug

        and

Crydon.

    Women.

Fanny Elliott

Mrs Humbug

    and

Daphne —

142

Act the First

Scene the 1st

A Garden.

Enter Corydon.

Cory:/ But Hush! I am interrupted.

(Exit Corydon

Enter Old Humbug & his Son, talking

Old Hum:/ It is for that reason I wish you
to follow my advice. Are you convin
of its propriety?

Young Hum:/ I am Sir, and will certainly
act in the manner you have pointed
out to me.

Old Hum:/ Then let us return to the Hou

(Exeunt)

Scene the 2.

A Parlour in Humbug's house.

Mrs Humbug & Fanny, discovered at work.

Mrs Hum:) You understand me my Love?

Fanny) Perfectly ma'am. Pray continue
    your narration.

Mrs Hum:) Alas! it is nearly concluded,
    for I have nothing more to say on the
    Subject.

Fanny) Ah! here's Daphne.

    Enter Daphne.

Daphne) My dear Mrs Humbug how dye
    do? oh! Fanny 'tis all over.

Fanny) Is it indeed!

Mrs Hum:) I'm very sorry to hear it.

Fanny/ Then t'was to no purpose that I . . . .

Daphne/ None upon Earth.

Mrs Hum:/ And what is to become of? . . . .

Daphne/ oh! thats all settled. (whispers Mrs Hum

Fanny/ And how is it determined?

Daphne/ I'll tell you. (whispers Fanny)

Mrs Hum:/ And is he to? . . .

Daphne/ I'll tell you all I know of the matter

(whispers Mrs Humbug & Fanny)

Fanny/ Well! now I know every thing about
       away.
it, I'll go ~~and stuff~~.

Mrs Hum:/
Daphne/ And so will I.

(Exeunt)

Scene the 3.

   The Curtain rises and discovers Sir Edu
Spangle reclined in an elegant Attitude on a

...a, fast asleep.

Enter Colonel Elliott.

Colonel) My Daughter is not here I see ... there
lies Sir Edward ... Shall I tell him the
secret? ... No, he'll certainly blab it ...
But he is asleep and wont hear one ... So
I'le een venture.

(Goes up to Sir Edward, whispers him, &
Exit)

End of the 1st Act.

Finis.

To Edward Austen Esqre

The following unfinished Novel

is respectfully inscribed

by

His obedient hum^{ble} Servt

The Author

The Three Sisters
a novel.

Letter 1st

Miss Stanhope to Mrs ——

My dear Fanny

I am the happiest creature in the
world, for I have just received an offer of mar=
=riage from Mr Watts. It is the first I have
ever had & I hardly know how to value it
enough. How I will triumph over the Duttons!
I do not intend to accept it, at least I beleive
not, but as I am not quite certain I gave
him an equivocal answer & left him.
And now my dear Fanny I want your
advice whether I should accept his offer or
not, but that you may be able to judge of
his merits & the situation of affairs I will
give you an account of them. He is quite
an old Man, about two & thirty, very plain
so plain that I cannot bear to look at him.
He is extremely disagreable & I hate him
more than any body else in the world. He has

a large fortune & will make great settlem
on me; but then he is very healthy. In sh
I do not know what to do. If I refuse h
he as good as told me that he should offe
himself to Sophia & if she refused him to
-giana, & I could not bear to have either
them married before me. If I accept hi
I know I shall be miserable all the rest
my life, for he is very ill tempered & peev
extremely jealous, & so stingy that there
no living in the house with him. He to
me he should mention the affair to Mam
but I insisted upon it that he did not f
very likely she would make me marry h
whether I would or no; however probably sh
has before now, for he never does anythi
he is desired to do. I believe I shall mar
him. It will be such a triumph to b
married before Sophy, Georgiana & the Du
And he promised to have a new Carriag
on the occasion, but we almost quarrell
about the colour, for I insisted upon its be
blue spotted with silver, & he declared it
should be a plain Chocolate; & to prov
me more said it should be just as low as

149

one. I wont have him I declare. He said he should come again tomorrow & take my final answer, so I believe I must get him while I can. I know the Duttons will envy me & I shall be able to chaperone Sophy & Georgiana to all the winter Balls. But then what will be the use of that when very likely he wont let me go myself, for I know he hates dancing & ~~has a great~~ ~~dislike of those things for himself~~ what he hates himself he has no idea of any other person's liking; & besides he ~~has a great idea~~ takes a great deal of Women's ways staying at home & such stuff. I believe I shant have him; I would refuse him at once if I were certain that neither of my Sisters would accept him, & that if they did not, he would not offer to the Duttons. I cannot run such a risk, if he will promise to have the Carriage ordered I like, I will have him, if not he may ride it by himself for me. I hope you like my termination; I can think of nothing better, And am your ever affec.te

Mary Stanhope

From the same to the Same

Dear Fanny

    I had but just sealed my last letter to you when my Mother came up & told me she wanted to speak to me on a very particular subject.

    "Ah! I know what you mean; (said I) That old fool Mr Watts has told you all about it, tho' I bid him not. However you shant force me to have him if I dont like it."

    "I am not going to force you Child, but only to know what your resolution is with regard to his Proposals, & to insist upon your making up your mind one way or t'other, if you dont accept him Sophy may."

    "Indeed (replied I hastily) Sophy need not trouble herself for I shall certainly marry myself."

    "If that is your resolution (said my Mother) why should you be afraid of my forcing you clinations?"

"Why, because I have not settled whether I shall have him or not."

"You are the strangest girl in the world Mary. What you say one moment, you unsay the next. Tell me once for all, whether you intend to marry Mr Watts or not?"

"Law Mama how can I tell you what I do not know myself?"

"Then I desire you will know, & quickly for Mr Watts says he wont be kept in sus— —nse."

"That depends upon me."

"No it does not, for if you do not give him a final answer tomorrow when he drinks tea with us, he intends to pay his addresses to Sophy."

"Then I shall tell all the world that he be: haved very ill to me."

"What good will that do? Mr Watts has been too long abused by all the world to mind it now."

"I wish I had a Father or a Brother becau[se] then they should fight him."

"They would be cunning if they did, for Watts would run away first; & therefore y[ou] must & shall resolve either to accept or re[fuse] him before tomorrow evening."

"But why if I don't have him, must [I] offer to my Sisters?"

"Why! Because he wishes to be allied to t[he] Family & because they are as pretty as you[."]

"But will Sophy marry him Mama if [he] offers to her?"

"Most likely. Why should not she? If how ever she does not choose it, then Georgia[na] must, for I am determined not to let suc[h] an opportunity escape of settling one of [my] Daughters so advantageously. So, make [the] most of your time; I leave you to settle [the] Matter with yourself." And then she went away. The only thing I can think of my de[ar]

...unny is to ask Sophy & Georgiana whether they
...uld have him were he to make proposals to
...m, & if they say they would not I am re-
...loved to refuse him too, for I hate him more
...an you can imagine. As for the Duttons
...he marries one of them I shall still have
...e triumph of having refused him first.
...adieu my dear Friend — Yrs ever M S.

Miss Georgiana Stanhope to Miss × × ×

Wednesday

dear Anne

    Sophy & I have just been practising
...ittle deceit on our eldest sister, to which
...are not perfectly reconciled, & yet the circum-
...nces were such that if any thing will
...use it, they must. Our neighbour Mr Watts
... made proposals to Mary; Proposals which
... knew not how to receive, for tho' she has a
...ticular Dislike to him (in which she is not
...gular) yet she would willingly marry him

sooner than risk his offering to Sophy or me
which in case of a refusal from herself
told her <del>he should do</del> he should do, for you must have
that the poor girl considers our marrying
before her as one of the greatest misfortune
that can possibly befall her, & to prevent
would willingly ensure herself everlasting
misery by a marriage with Mr Watts. An
hour ago she came to us to sound our in
:nations respecting the affair which we
to determine hers. A little before she
came my Mother had given us an a
:count of it, telling us that she certa
:ly would not let him go farther tha
our family for a Wife." "And therefore (sa
she) If Mary wont have him Sophy must
if Sophy wont Georgiana shall." Poor Ge
:giana! — We neither of us attempted
alter my Mother's resolution, which I
sorry to say is generally more strictly
than rationally formed. As soon as sh
was gone however I broke silence to
assure Sophy that if Mary should ref
Mr Watts I should not expect her to

...ifice her happiness by becoming his
...ife from a motive of Generosity to me,
...hich I was afraid her Goodnature and
...isterly affection might induce her to do.
"Let us flatter ourselves (replied she) that
...ary will not refuse him. Yet how can
...ope that my Sister may accept a Man
...ho cannot make her happy."

"He cannot it is true — but his Fortune
...s Name, his House, his Carriage will
...nd I have no doubt but that Mary will
...arry him; indeed why should she not?
...e is not more than two & thirty; a
...ry proper age for a Man to marry at;
... is rather plain to be sure, but then
...hat is Beauty in a Man; if he has
...t a genteel figure & a sensible looking
...ce it is quite sufficient."

"This is all very true Georgiana but Mr
...atts's figure is unfortunately extremely vul:
...ar & his Countenance is very heavy."

"And then as to his temper; it has been
...houed bad, but may not the World be deceived
...their Judgement of it. There is an open

Frankness in his Disposition which be[c...]
a Man; They say he is stingy; I will ca[ll]
that Prudence. They say he is suspiciou[s]
That proceeds from a warmth of Hear[t]
always excusable in Youth, & inshort [I]
see no reason why he should not mak[e a]
very good Husband, or why Mary should
not be very happy with him."

Sophy laughed; I continued,

"However whether Mary accepts hi[m]
or not I am resolved. My determination
made. I never would marry Mr Watts wer[e]
Beggary the only alternative. So deficie[nt]
in every respect! Hideous in his person [&]
without one good Quality to make amen[ds]
for it. His fortune to be sure is good." Ye[t]
not so very large! Three thousand a yea[r]
What is three thousand a year? It is bu[t]
six times as much as my Mother's in
-come. It will not tempt me."

"Yet it will be a noble fortune for [you,"]
said Sophy laughing again.

"For Mary! Yes indeed it will give m[e]

...easure to see her in such affluence."

...us I ran on to the great Entertainment

...my Sister, till Mary came into the room

...appearance in great agitation. she sate

...un. We made room for her at the fire.

...e seemed at a loss how to begin & at last

...id in some confusion

"Pray Sophy have you any mind to be

...arried?"

"To be married! none in the least. But why

...you ask me? are you acquainted with any

...e who means to make me proposals?"

"I— no, how should I? But mayn't I ask a

...mmon question?"

"Not a very common one Mary surely. (said

...e paused & after some moments silence

...ent on—

"How should you like to marry Mr Watts

...phy?"

...winked at Sophy & replied for her. "Who is

...ere but must rejoice to marry a man

...f three thousand a year; ~~who keeps a post~~

~~chaise & pair, with silver Harness~~

~~before~~ ~~to look out about~~

"Very true (she replied) That's very true.
you would have him if he would offer, Ge
-graina, & would you Sophy?"

Sophy did not like the idea of telling a
lie & deceiving her Sister; she prevented the
first & saved half her conscience by equi
-vocation.

"I should certainly act just as Georgia
would do."

"Well then said Mary with triumph in
Eyes, I have had an offer from Mr Watson
we were of course very much surprised
do not accept him said I, and then perha
he may have me."

In short my scheme took & Mary is re
solved to do that to prevent our suppos
happiness which she would not have
to ~~have made~~ cause it in reality. Yet after all
Heart cannot acquit me & Sophy is eve
more scrupulous. Quiet our Minds my G
lenne by writing & telling us you appro
our conduct. Consider it well over. Ma

e have real pleasure in beeing a married
man, & able to chaprone us, which she cer-
inly shall do, for I think myself bound to
ribute as much as possible to her happiness
a state I have made her choose. They
e probably have a new Carriage, which
l be paradise to her, & if we can prevail
Mr W. to set up his Phaeton she will
too happy. These things however would
no consolation to Sophy or me for domestic
ery. Remember all this & do not con—
mn us.

Friday.

st night Mr Watts by appointment
nk tea with us. As soon as his Carriage
ped at the Door, Mary went to the Window.
uld you beleive it Sophy (said she) the old
l wants to have his new Chaise just
colour of the old one, & hung as low too.
l it shant—I will carry my point. And if he
t let it be as high as the Duttons, & blue
ted with silver, I wont have him. Yes I
too. Here he comes. I know he'le be rude;
now he'le be illtempered & wont say one

civil thing to me! nor behave at all like
Lover." She then sate down & Mr Watts enter

"Ladies your most obedient." We paid ou
Compliments & he seated himself.

"Fine Weather Ladies." Then turning to Ma
"Well Miss Stanhope I hope you have at le
settled the Matter in your own mind; & wo
be so good as to let me know whether you
will condescend to marry me or not."

"I think Sir (said Mary) You might ha
asked in a genteeler way than that. I do
know whether I shall have you if you beh
so odd."

"Mary!" (said my Mother) "well Mar
if he will be so cross.....

"Hush, hush, Mary, you shall not be
to Mr Watts."

"Pray Madam do not lay any restraint
Miss Stanhope by obliging her to be civil..
She does not choose to accept my hand, I
offer it else where, for as I am by no mea
guided by a particular preference to y

ve your sisters it is equally the same to me which I marry of the three." Was there ever such wretch! Sophy reddened with anger, & I felt so ...eful!

...ell then (said Mary in a peevish accent) ...ile have you if I must."

...should have thought Miss Stanhope ...t when such settlements are offered as ...ve offered to you there can be no great ...ence done to the inclinations in accepting ...em."

...ry mumbled out something, which I who ...close to her could just distinguish to ...What's the use of a great Jointure if Men ...forever?" and then audibly "Remember ...pin money; two hundred a year."

...hundred & seventy five Madam."

...o hundred indeed Sir" said my Mother.

...nd Remember I am to have a new Carri— ...being as high as the Duttons', & blue ...ted with silver; and I shall expect a ...saddle horse, a suit of fine lace, and an ...ite Number of the most valuable Jewels. Diamonds

such as never were seen! ~~People at large with~~
~~of the Princes Ball all~~ and ~~in the~~ ~~Bridel~~
~~of the~~ and Pearls, Rubies, Emeralds
~~Sapphires, amethyst, Turkey stones, Agates,~~ ~~Pearls~~
~~Pearls of~~ and Beads out of number. You must set
up your Phaeton which must be cream colour
with a wreath of silver flowers round it, You
must buy 4 of the finest Bays in the Kingdom
& you must drive me in it every day. This is
not all; You must entirely new furnish your
House after my Taste, You must hire two more
Footmen to attend me, two Women to wait on me,
must always let me do just as I please and be
a very good husband."

Here she stopped, I believe rather out of breath.
"This is all very reasonable Mr Watts for my
Daughter to expect."

"And it is very reasonable Mrs Stanhope
that your daughter should be disappointed."
He was going on but Mary interrupted him
"You must build me an elegant Greenhouse
& stock it with plants. You must let me
spend every Winter in Bath, every Spring
in Town, Every Summer in taking some Tour

d every autumn at a Watering Place, and if 63
are at home the rest of the year (Sophy & I laugh)
you must do nothing but give Balls and
Masquerades. You must build a room on purpose
& a Theatre to act Plays in. The first Play we
have shall be Which is the Man and I will
Lady Bell Bloomer."

"And pray Miss Stanhope (said Mr Watts)
what am I to expect from you in return for
this."

"Expect? why you may expect to have me pleas
"

"It would be odd if I did not. Your expectations
Madam are too high for me, & I must apply to
Miss Sophy who perhaps may not have raise
'em so much."

"You are mistaken Sir in supposing so, (said
Sophy) for tho' they may not be exactly in the
same Line, yet my expectations are to the full
as high as my Sister's; for I expect my Husband
to be good tempered & Chearful; to consult my
happiness in all his actions, & to love me
with Constancy & Sincerity."

Mr Watts stared. "These are very odd Ideas

truly young Lady. You had better discard them
:fore you marry, or you will be obliged to do it af
-terwards."

My Mother in the meantime was lecturi
Mary who was sensible that she had gone
too far, &, when Mr Watts was just turnin
towards me in order I believe to address me,
spoke to him in a voice half humble, half sulky

"You are mistaken Mr Watts if you thin
I was in earnest when I said I expected so
much. However I must have a new Chais

"Yes Sir, you must allow that Mary ha
a right to expect that."

"Mrs Stanhope, I mean — & have always
meant to have a new one on my Marri
But it shall be the colour of my presen
one."

"I think Mr Watts you should pay my da
the compliment of consulting her Tast
on such Matters."

Mr Watts would not agree to this, & for
time insisted upon its being a Chocolate colou
while Mary was as eager for having it blue w
silver Spots. At length however Sophy propos

165

...t to please Mr W. It should be a dark brown to please Mary it should be hung rather high ...ave a silver Border. This was at length ...ed to, tho' reluctantly on both sides, as each ...intended to carry their point entire. We then ...eeded to other Matters, & it was settled that ...y should be married as soon as the Writings could ...completed. Mary was very eager for a special ...nce & Mr Watts talked of Banns. A common ...nce was at last agreed on. Mary is to have ...the Family Jewels which are very inconside- ...ble I believe & Mr W. promised to buy her a ...dle horse; but in return she is not to expect ...s to Town or any other public place for thise ...e Years. She is to have neither Greenhouse, ...ate or Phaeton; to be contented with one Maid ...hout an additional Footman. It engrossed the ...le Evening to settle these affairs; Mr W. supped ...h us & did not go till twelve. As soon as he ...gone Mary exclaimed "Thank Heaven! he's off ...ast; how I do hate him!" It was in vain ...t Mama represented to her the impropriety ...was guilty of in disliking him who was ...e her Husband, for she persisted in declaring ...cession to him & hoping she might never ...him again. What a Wedding will this be! ...n my dear Anne - Yr faithfully Sincere
Georgiana Stanhope

From the Same to the Same

Dear Anne   Saturday

     Mary eager to have every one know of her
approaching Wedding & more particularly desirous
of triumphing as she called it over the Dutto—
desired us to walk with her this morning to S—
ham. As we had nothing else to do we read—
agreed, & had as pleasant a walk as we could
have with Mary whose conversation entirely consist—
in abusing the Man she is so soon to marry &
in longing for a blue Chaise spotted with Silver
When we reached the Duttons we found the
two Girls in the dressing-room with a very
handsome Young Man, who was of course in—
-duced to us. He is the son of Sir Henry Bru—
-nell of Leicestershire. ~~And as I to to the Tum~~
~~~~~~~~~~~~~~~~~~~~~~~~~~ ~~His~~
~~Sister is ~~~~~~ to John ~~~~~~~~~~~~~~ Bu~~
~~~~~~~~~~~~~~~~~~~~~~~~~~~~~~~~~~~~ he~~
~~~~~~~~~~~~~~~~~~~~~~~~~~~~~~~~~~ Mr Bruden~~
is the handsomest Man I ever saw in m—
Life; we are all three very much pleas—
with him. Mary, who from the moment of
our reaching the Dressing room had been

...elling with the knowledge of her own impot 77
...nce & with the Desire of making it known,
...d not remain long silent on the Subject after
...were seated, & soon addressing herself to Kitty
...d,

"Dont you think it will be necessary to have
... the Jewels new set?"

"Necessary for what?"

"What! Why for my appearance.   "

"...beg your pardon but I really do not under
...nd you. What Jewels do you speak of, and
...re is your appearance to be made?"

"...t the next Ball to be sure after I am mar —
...d."

"...ou may imagine their Surprise. They were
...first incredulous, but on our joining in
... Story they at last believed it. "And who is
...?" was of course the first Question. Mary
...tended Bashfulness, & answered in Confusion
...Eyes cast down "to Mr Watts". This also
...ived Confirmation from us, for that anyone
...o had the Beauty & fortune (tho' small) yet a
...rison) of Mary would willingly marry Mr
                                        Watts,

could by them scarcely be credited. The subj being now fairly introduced and she found herself the object of everyone's attention in c -pany, she lost all her confusion & became perfectly unreserved & communicative.

"I wonder you should never have heard of it before for in general things of this natu are very well known in the neighbourhood.

"I assure you said Jemima I never had the least suspicion of such an affair. Has it been in agitation long?"

"Oh! Yes, ever since Wednesday."
They all smiled particularly Mr Brudenell.

"You must know Mr Watts is very much in love with me, so that it is quite a ma of affection on his side."

"not on his only, I suppose" said Kitty.

"Oh! When there is so much love on one sid there is no occasion for it on the other. How I do not much dislike him tho' he is very plain to be sure."

Mr Brudenell stared, the Miss Duttons la

169

...phy & I were heartily ashamed of our Sis...
... She went on.

...e are to have a new Post chaise and very
...ly may set up our Phaeton."

...is we knew to be false but the poor girl
...s pleased at the idea of perswading the com—
...any that such a thing was to be & I would
... deprive her of so harmless an Enjoyment.
... continued.

...Watts is to present me with the family
...ls which I fancy are very considerable."
...ld not help whispering Sophy "I fancy not."
...se Jewels are what I suppose must be
...set before they can be worn. I shall not wear
...m till the first Ball I go to after my Mar—
...e. If Mrs Dutton should not go to it, I hope
... will let me chaprone you; I shall certain...
...take Sophy & Georgiana."

...You are very good (said Kitty) & since you
... inclined to undertake the care of young
...dies, I should advise you to prevail on Mrs
...icumbe to let you chaprone her six Daughters
...ch with your two sisters and ourselves will

make your Entrée very respectable."

Kitty made us all smile except Mary who
did not understand her Meaning & coolly
that she should not like to chaprone so many

Sophy & I now endeavoured to change the co
-versation but succeeded only for a few Minu
for Mary took care to bring back their atte
-tion to her & her approaching Wedding.
I was sorry for my Sister's sake to see tha
Mr Brudenell seemed to take pleasure in
listening to her account of it, & even en
couraged her ~~in doing so~~ by his Questions
& Remarks, for it was evident that his on
Aim was to laugh at her. I am afraid
he found her very ridiculous. He kept his
Countenance extremely well, yet it was
easy to see that it was with difficulty
he kept it. At length however he seemed
-tigued & Disgusted with her ridiculous Con
-versation, as he turned from her to us, & spo
but little to her for about half an hour be
we left Stoneham. As soon as we were ou
of the House we all joined in praising the

on & Manners of Mr Brudenell.

e found Mr Watts at home.

, Miss Stanhope (said he) you see I am come
urting in a true lover like Manner."

"Well you need not have told me that. I knew
y you came very well."

Sophy & I then left the room, imagining of
se that we must be in the way, if a
ne of Courtship were to begin. We were sur-
ised at being followed almost immediately
Mary.

nd is your Courting so soon over?" said Sophy

ourting! (replied Mary) we have been quar-
elling. Watts is such a Fool! I hope I shall
er see him again."

am afraid you will, (said I) as he dines here
day. But what has been your dispute?"

ly only because I told him that I had seen
an much handsomer than he was this
ning, he flew into a great Passion & called
a Vixen, so I only stayed to tell him I thought
a Blackguard & came away."

"Short & sweet, (said Sophy,) but pray Mary how
will be this be made up?"

"He ought to ask my pardon; but if he did, I
would not forgive him."

"His submission then would not be unnecessary.
When we were dressed we returned to the
Parlour where Mama & Mr Watts were in close
Conversation. It seems that he had been complaining to her of her Daughter's behaviour
& she had persuaded him to think no more
He therefore met Mary with all his accustomed
Civility, & except one touch at the Phaeton and
another at the Greenhouse, the Evening went
off with great Harmony & Cordiality. Watts is
going to Town to hasten the preparations for
the Wedding. I am your affec:te Freind G.S.

173

To Miss Jane Anna Elizabeth Austen

My Dear Neice

Though you are at this period not many degrees removed from Infancy, Yet trusting that you will in time be older, and that through the care of your excellent Parents, you will one day or another be able to read written hand, I dedicate to You the following Miscellaneous Morsels, convinced that if you seriously attend to them, You will derive from them very important Instructions, with regard to your Conduct in Life.— If such my hopes should hereafter be realized, never will I regret the Days and Nights that have been spent in composing these Treatises for your Benefit—. I am my dear Neice

Your very Affectionate
Aunt.
The Author.

June 2d
1793—

A fragment ~~a written to inculcate the~~ practice of Virtue.

We all know that many are unfortunate in their progress through the world, but do not know all that are so. To seek them, to study their wants, & to leave them unsupplied is the duty, and ought to be the Business of Man. But few have time, fewer still have inclination, and no one has either the one or the other for such employments. Who are those that perspire away their evenings in crowded assemblies can trace leisure to bestow thought on such as sweat under the fatigue of their daily Labour.

A beautiful description of the different
... of Sensibility on different Minds.

_____

I am but just returned from Melissa's
... side, & in my life tho' it has been a pretty
... one, & I have during the course of it been
... many Bedsides, I never saw so affecting an
... as she exhibits. She lies wrapped in a
... muslin bedgown, a chambray gauze shift
... a french net nightcap. Sir William is con:
...antly at her bedside. The only repose he
... is on the Sopha in the Drawing room,
... for five minutes every fortnight he
...ains in an imperfect Slumber, starting
... every moment & exclaiming "Oh! Melissa,
...! Melissa," then sinking down again, raises
... left arm and scratches his head. Poor Mrs
...maby is beyond measure afflicted. She sighs
... now and then, that is about once a
...ek; which the melancholy Charles says every

moment, "Melissa how are you?" The lovely
:ters are much to be pitied. Julia is ever la
:menting the situation of her friend, while
behind her pillow & supporting her head — Ya
more mild in her grief talks of going to To
next week, and Anna is always recurring
the pleasures we once enjoyed when Melissa
well. — I am usually at the fire cooking
little delicacy for the unhappy invalid —
:haps hashing up the remains of an old &
tasting some cheese, or making a curry w
are the favourite dishes of our poor friend.
In these situations we were this morning
:prised by receiving a visit from Dr Dowkin
"I am come to see Melissa" said he. "How is
"Very weak indeed, said the fainting Mely
"Very weak, replied the punning Doctor, a
indeed it is more than a very week si
you have taken to your bed — How is yo

netite?" "Bad, very bad, said Julia."

t is very bad — replied he. Are her spirits
d Madam?" "So poorly Sir that we are ob-
d to strengthen her with cordials every
ute." — "Well then she receives Spirits
m your being with her. Does she sleep?
arcely ever —. "And Ever Scarcely I suppose
hen she does. Poor thing! Does she think
dieing? "She has not strength to think
all. "Nay then she cannot think to have
ngth."

The Generous Curate —
a moral Tale, setting forth the
Advantages of being Generous and a Curate.

In a part little known of the County of
---- , a very worthy Clergyman lately
died. The income of his living which amount-
to about two hundred pound, & the interest
his Wife's fortune which was nothing at all

was entirely sufficient for the wants & wis.
of a Family who neither wanted or wished f
anything beyond what their income afforded.
Mr Williams had been in possession of his liv
above twenty years, when their history commen
& his Marriage which had taken place soon a
his presentation to it, had made him the fa
of six very fine Children. The eldest had been,
at the Royal Academy for Seamen at Portsmou
when about thirteen years old, and from then
had been discharged on board of one of the Vess
of a small fleet destined for Newfoundland, w
his promising & amiable disposition had procu
him many friends among the Natives, & from w.
he regularly sent home a large Newfoundland D
every Month to his family. The second, who w
also a Son had been adopted by a neighbour
Clergyman with the intention of educating hi
at his own expence, which would have be
a very desirable Circumstance had the Gentle

...ture been equal to his generosity, but as he
...nothing to support himself and a very large
...ily but a curacy of fifty pound a year, young
...lians knew nothing more at the age of 18 than
...a twopenny Dame's School in the village could
...h him. His Character however was perfectly
...iable though his genius might be cramped,
...d he was addicted to no vice, or ever guilty of
...fault beyond what his age and situation
...dered perfectly excusable. He had indeed some:
...ies been detected in flinging Stones at a Duck
...rutting brickbats into his Benefactor's bed; but
...se innocent efforts of wit were considered
...that good man rather as the effects of a lively
...agination, than of anything bad in his nature,
...d if any punishment were decreed for the of:
...nce it was in general no greater than that
...Culprit should pick up the Stones or take
...brickbats away. —

Finis

To Miss Austen, the following Ode to Pity
is dedicated, from a thorough knowledge of her
pitiful Nature, by her obed.t hum:le Serv.t

The Author

Ode to Pity

1

Ever musing I delight to tread
   The Paths of honour and the Myrtle Grove
Whilst the pale Moon her beams doth shed
   On disappointed Love.
While Philomel on airy hawthorn Bush
   Sings sweet & Melancholy, And the thrush
Converses with the Dove.

2.

Gently brawling down the turnpike road,
   Sweetly noisy falls the silent Stream —
The Moon emerges from behind a Cloud
   And darts upon the Myrtle Grove her beam.
Ah! then what Lovely Scenes appear,
   The hut, the Cot, the Grot, & Chapel queer,
And eke the Abbey too a mouldering heap,
   Conceal'd by aged pines her head doth rear
And quite invisible doth take a peep.

End of the first volume.   June 3 1793

(IV + 180 pages)

VOLUME THE FIRST

———

CONTENTS

To Miss Lloyd

MY DEAR MARTHA

    As a small testimony of the gratitude I feel for your late generosity to me in finishing my muslin Cloak, I beg leave to offer you this little production of your sincere Freind

THE AUTHOR

Frederic & Elfrida

A Novel

CHAPTER THE FIRST

The Uncle of Elfrida was the Father of Frederic; in other words, they were first cousins by the Father's side.

Being both born in one day & both brought up at one school, it was not wonderfull that they should look on each other with something more than bare politeness. They loved with mutual sincerity but were both determined not to transgress the rules of Propriety by owning their attachment, either to the object beloved, or to any one else.

They were exceedingly handsome and so much alike, that it was not every one who knew them apart. Nay even their most intimate freinds had nothing to distinguish them by, but the shape of the face, the colour of the Eye, the length of the Nose & the difference of the complexion.

Elfrida had an intimate freind to whom, being on a visit to an Aunt, she wrote the following Letter.

TO MISS DRUMMOND

DEAR CHARLOTTE

I should be obliged to you, if you would buy me, during your stay with Mrs Williamson, a new & fashionable Bonnet, to suit the complexion of your

E. FALKNOR

Charlotte, whose character was a willingness to oblige every one, when she returned into the Country, brought her Freind the wished-for Bonnet, & so ended this little adventure, much to the satisfaction of all parties.

On her return to Crankhumdunberry (of which sweet village her father was Rector) Charlotte was received with the greatest Joy by Frederic & Elfrida, who, after pressing her alternately to their Bosoms, proposed to her to take a walk in a Grove of Poplars which led from the Parsonage to a verdant Lawn enamelled with a variety of variegated flowers & watered by a purling Stream, brought from the Valley of Tempé by a passage under ground.

In this Grove they had scarcely remained above 9 hours, when they were suddenly agreably surprized by hearing a most delightfull voice warble the following stanza.

SONG

That Damon was in love with me
I once thought & beleiv'd
But now that he is not I see,
I fear I was deceiv'd.

No sooner were the lines finished than they beheld by a turning in the Grove 2 elegant young women leaning on each other's arm, who immediately on perceiving them, took a different path & disappeared from their sight.

CHAPTER THE SECOND

As Elfrida & her companions, had seen enough of them to know that they were neither the 2 Miss Greens, nor Mrs Jackson and her Daughter, they could not help expressing their surprise at their appearance; till at length recollecting, that a new family had lately taken a House not far from the Grove, they hastened home, determined to lose no time in forming an acquaintance with 2 such amiable & worthy Girls, of which family they rightly imagined them to be a part.

Agreable to such a determination, they went that very evening to pay their respects to Mrs Fitzroy & her two Daughters. On being shewn into an elegant dressing room, ornamented with festoons of artificial flowers, they were struck with the engaging Exterior & beautifull outside of Jezalinda the eldest of the young Ladies; but e'er they had been many minutes seated, the Wit & Charms which shone resplendent in the conversation of the amiable Rebecca, enchanted them so much that they all with one accord jumped up and exclaimed.

"Lovely & too charming Fair one, notwithstanding your forbidding Squint, your greazy tresses & your swelling Back, which are more frightfull than imagination can paint or pen describe, I cannot refrain from expressing my raptures, at the engaging Qualities of your Mind, which so amply atone for the Horror, with which your first appearance must ever inspire the unwary visitor."

"Your sentiments so nobly expressed on the different excellencies of Indian & English Muslins, & the judicious preference you give the former, have excited in me an admiration of which I can alone give an adequate idea, by assuring you it is nearly equal to what I feel for myself."

Then making a profound Curtesy to the amiable & abashed Rebecca, they left the room & hurried home.

From this period, the intimacy between the Families of Fitzroy, Drummond, and Falknor, daily increased till at length it grew to such a pitch, that they did not scruple to kick one another out of the window on the slightest provocation.

During this happy state of Harmony, the eldest Miss Fitzroy ran off with the Coachman & the amiable Rebecca was asked in marriage by Captain Roger of Buckinghamshire.

Mrs Fitzroy did not approve of the match on account of the tender years of the young couple, Rebecca being but 36 & Captain Roger little more than 63. To remedy this objection, it was agreed that they should wait a little while till they were a good deal older.

CHAPTER THE THIRD

In the mean time the parents of Frederic proposed to those of Elfrida, an union between them, which being accepted with pleasure, the wedding cloathes were bought & nothing remained to be settled but the naming of the Day.

As to the lovely Charlotte, being importuned with eagerness to pay another visit to her Aunt, she determined to accept the invitation & in consequence of it walked to Mrs Fitzroys to take leave of the amiable Rebecca, whom she found surrounded by Patches, Powder, Pomatum & Paint with which she was vainly endeavouring to remedy the natural plainness of her face.

"I am come my amiable Rebecca, to take my leave of you for the fortnight I am destined to spend with my aunt. Beleive me this separation is painfull to me, but it is as necessary as the labour which now engages you."

"Why to tell you the truth my Love, replied Rebecca, I have lately taken it into my head to think (perhaps with little reason) that my complexion is by no means equal to the rest of my face & have therefore taken, as you see, to white & red paint which I would scorn to use on any other occasion as I hate art."

Charlotte, who perfectly understood the meaning of her freind's speech, was too good-temper'd & obliging to refuse her, what she knew she wished,—a compliment; & they parted the best freinds in the world.

With a heavy heart & streaming Eyes did she ascend the lovely vehicle[1] which bore her from her freinds & home; but greived as she was, she little thought in what a strange & different manner she should return to it.

On her entrance into the city of London which was the place of Mrs Williamson's abode, the postilion, whose stupidity was amazing, declared & declared even without the least shame or Compunction, that having never been informed he was totally ignorant of what part of the Town, he was to drive to.

Charlotte, whose nature we have before intimated, was an earnest desire to oblige every one, with the greatest Condescension & Goodhumour informed him that he was to drive to Portland Place, which he accordingly did & Charlotte soon found herself in the arms of a fond Aunt.

Scarcely were they seated as usual, in the most affectionate manner in one chair,

---

[1] a post-chaise.

than the Door suddenly opened & an aged gentleman with a sallow face & old pink Coat, partly by intention & partly thro' weakness was at the feet of the lovely Charlotte, declaring his attachment to her & beseeching her pity in the most moving manner.

Not being able to resolve to make any one miserable, she consented to become his wife; where upon the Gentleman left the room & all was quiet.

Their quiet however continued but a short time, for on a second opening of the door a young & Handsome Gentleman with a new blue coat, entered & intreated from the lovely Charlotte, permission to pay to her, his addresses.

There was a something in the appearance of the second Stranger, that influenced Charlotte in his favour, to the full as much as the appearance of the first: she could not account for it, but so it was.

Having therefore agreable to that & the natural turn of her mind to make every one happy, promised to become his Wife the next morning, he took his leave & the two Ladies sat down to Supper on a young Leveret, a brace of Partridges, a leash of Pheasants & a Dozen of Pigeons.

CHAPTER THE FOURTH

It was not till the next morning that Charlotte recollected the double engagement she had entered into; but when she did, the reflection of her past folly, operated so strongly on her mind, that she resolved to be guilty of a greater, & to that end threw herself into a deep stream which ran thro' her Aunt's pleasure Grounds in Portland Place.

She floated to Crankhumdunberry where she was picked up & buried; the following epitaph, composed by Frederick Elfrida & Rebecca, was placed on her tomb.

EPITAPH

> Here lies our friend who having promis-ed
> That unto two she would be marri-ed
> Threw her sweet Body & her lovely face
> Into the Stream that runs thro' Portland Place.

These sweet lines, as pathetic as beautifull were never read by any one who passed that way, without a shower of tears, which if they should fail of exciting in you, Reader, your mind must be unworthy to peruse them.

Having performed the last sad office to their departed freind, Frederic & Elfrida together with Captain Roger & Rebecca returned to Mrs Fitzroy's at whose feet they threw themselves with one accord & addressed her in the following Manner.

"MADAM"

"When the sweet Captain Roger first addressed the amiable Rebecca, you alone objected to their union on account of the tender years of the Parties. That plea can be no more, seven days being now expired, together with the lovely Charlotte, since the Captain first spoke to you on the subject."

"Consent then Madam to their union & as a reward, this smelling Bottle which I enclose in my right hand, shall be yours & yours forever; I never will claim it again. But if you refuse to join their hands in 3 days time, this dagger which I enclose in my left shall be steeped in your hearts blood."

"Speak then Madam & decide their fate & yours."

Such gentle & sweet persuasion could not fail of having the desired effect. The answer they received, was this.

"MY DEAR YOUNG FREINDS"

"The arguments you have used are too just & too eloquent to be withstood; Rebecca in 3 days time, you shall be united to the Captain."

This speech, than which nothing could be more satisfactory, was received with Joy by all; & peace being once more restored on all sides, Captain Roger intreated Rebecca to favour them with a Song, in compliance with which request having first assured them that she had a terrible cold, she sung as follows.

SONG

When Corydon went to the fair
He bought a red ribbon for Bess,
With which she encircled her hair
& made herself look very fess.

CHAPTER THE FIFTH

At the end of 3 days Captain Roger and Rebecca were united and immediately after the Ceremony set off in the Stage Waggon for the Captains seat in Buckinghamshire.

The parents of Elfrida, alltho' they earnestly wished to see her married to Frederic before they died, yet knowing the delicate frame of her mind could ill bear the least exertion & rightly judging that naming her wedding day would be too great a one, forebore to press her on the subject.

Weeks & Fortnights flew away without gaining the least ground; the Cloathes grew out of fashion & at length Capt: Roger & his Lady arrived, to pay a visit to their Mother & introduce to her their beautifull Daughter of eighteen.

Elfrida, who had found her former acquaintance were growing too old & too ugly to be any longer agreable, was rejoiced to hear of the arrival of so pretty a girl as Eleanor with whom she determined to form the strictest freindship.

But the Happiness she had expected from an acquaintance with Eleanor, she soon found was not to be received, for she had not only the mortification of finding herself treated by her as little less than an old woman, but had actually the horror of perceiving a growing passion in the Bosom of Frederic for the Daughter of the amiable Rebecca.

The instant she had the first idea of such an attachment, she flew to Frederic & in a manner truly heroick, spluttered out to him her intention of being married the next Day.

To one in his predicament who possessed less personal Courage than Frederic was master of, such a speech would have been Death; but he not being the least terrified boldly replied.

"Damme Elfrida *you* may be married tomorrow but *I* wont."

This answer distressed her too much for her delicate Constitution. She accordingly fainted & was in such a hurry to have a succession of fainting fits, that she had scarcely patience enough to recover from one before she fell into another.

Tho', in any threatening Danger to his Life or Liberty, Frederic was as bold as brass yet in other respects his heart was as soft as cotton & immediately on hearing of the dangerous way Elfrida was in, he flew to her & finding her better than he had been taught to expect, was united to her Forever—.

FINIS

Jack & Alice

A Novel

Is respectfully inscribed to Francis William Austen Esqr Midshipman on board his Majesty's Ship the Perseverance by his obedient humble Servant The Author

CHAPTER THE FIRST

Mr Johnson was once upon a time about 53; in a twelvemonth afterwards he was 54, which so much delighted him that he was determined to celebrate his next Birthday by giving a Masquerade to his Children & Freinds. Accordingly on the Day he attained his 55th year tickets were dispatched to all his Neighbours to that purpose. His acquaintance indeed in that part of the World were not very numerous as they consisted only of Lady Williams, Mr & Mrs Jones, Charles Adams & the 3 Miss Simpsons, who composed the neighbourhood of Pammydiddle & formed the Masquerade.

Before I proceed to give an account of the Evening, it will be proper to describe to my reader, the persons and Characters of the party introduced to his acquaintance.

Mr & Mrs Jones were both rather tall & very passionate, but were in other respects, good tempered, wellbehaved People. Charles Adams was an amiable, accomplished & bewitching young Man; of so dazzling a Beauty that none but Eagles could look him in the Face.

Miss Simpson was pleasing in her person, in her Manners & in her Disposition; an unbounded ambition was her only fault. Her second sister Sukey was Envious, Spitefull & Malicious. Her person was short, fat & disagreable. Cecilia (the youngest) was perfectly handsome but too affected to be pleasing.

In Lady Williams every virtue met. She was a widow with a handsome Jointure & the remains of a very handsome face. Tho' Benevolent & Candid, she was Generous & sincere; Tho' Pious & Good, she was Religious & amiable, & Tho Elegant & Agreable, she was Polished & Entertaining.

The Johnsons were a family of Love, & though a little addicted to the Bottle & the Dice, had many good Qualities.

Such was the party assembled in the elegant Drawing Room of Johnson Court, amongst which the pleasing figure of a Sultana was the most remarkable of the female Masks. Of the Males a Mask representing the Sun, was the most universally admired. The Beams that darted from his Eyes were like those of that glorious Luminary tho' infinitely superior. So strong were they that no one dared venture within half a mile of them; he had therefore the best part of the Room to himself, its size not amounting to more than 3 quarters of a mile in length & half a one in breadth. The Gentleman at last finding the feirceness of his beams to be very inconvenient to the concourse by obliging them to croud together in one corner of the room, half shut his eyes by which means, the Company discovered him to be Charles Adams in his plain green Coat, without any mask at all.

When their astonishment was a little subsided their attention was attracted by 2 Domino's who advanced in a horrible Passion; they were both very tall, but seemed in other respects to have many good qualities. "These said the witty Charles, these are Mr & Mrs Jones." and so indeed they were.

No one could imagine who was the Sultana! Till at length on her addressing a beautifull Flora who was reclining in a studied attitude on a couch, with "Oh Cecilia, I wish I was really what I pretend to be", she was discovered by the never failing genius of Charles Adams, to be the elegant but ambitious Caroline Simpson, & the person to whom she addressed herself, he rightly imagined to be her lovely but affected sister Cecilia.

The Company now advanced to a Gaming Table where sat 3 Dominos (each with a bottle in their hand) deeply engaged; but a female in the character of Virtue fled with hasty footsteps from the shocking scene, whilst a little fat woman representing Envy, sate alternately on the foreheads of the 3 Gamesters. Charles Adams was still as bright as ever; he soon discovered the party at play to be the 3 Johnsons, Envy to be Sukey Simpson & Virtue to be Lady Williams.

The Masks were then all removed & the Company retired to another room, to partake of an elegant & well managed Entertainment, after which the Bottle being pretty briskly pushed about by the 3 Johnsons, the whole party not excepting even Virtue were carried home, Dead Drunk.

CHAPTER THE SECOND

For three months did the Masquerade afford ample subject for conversation to the inhabitants of Pammydiddle; but no character at it was so fully expatiated on as Charles Adams. The singularity of his appearance, the beams which darted from his eyes, the brightness of his Wit, & the whole *tout ensemble* of his person had subdued the hearts of so many of the young Ladies, that of the six present at the Masquerade but five had returned uncaptivated. Alice Johnson was the unhappy sixth whose heart had not been able to withstand the power of his Charms. But as it may appear strange to my Readers, that so much worth & Excellence as he possessed should have conquered only hers, it will be necessary to inform them that the Miss Simpsons were defended from his Power by Ambition, Envy, & Self-admiration.

Every wish of Caroline was centered in a titled Husband; whilst in Sukey such superior excellence could only raise her Envy not her Love, & Cecilia was too tenderly attached to herself to be pleased with any one besides. As for Lady Williams and Mrs Jones, the former of them was too sensible, to fall in love with one so much her Junior and the latter, tho' very tall & very passionate was too fond of her Husband to think of such a thing.

Yet in spite of every endeavour on the part of Miss Johnson to discover any attachment to her in him; the cold & indifferent heart of Charles Adams still to all appearance, preserved its native freedom; polite to all but partial to none, he still remained the lovely, the lively, but insensible Charles Adams.

One evening, Alice finding herself somewhat heated by wine (no very uncommon case) determined to seek a relief for her disordered Head & Love-sick Heart in the Conversation of the intelligent Lady Williams.

She found her Ladyship at home as was in general the Case, for she was not fond of going out, & like the great Sir Charles Grandison scorned to deny herself when at Home, as she looked on that fashionable method of shutting out disagreable Visitors, as little less than downright Bigamy.

In spite of the wine she had been drinking, poor Alice was uncommonly out of spirits; she could think of nothing but Charles Adams, she could talk of nothing but him, & in short spoke so openly that Lady Williams soon discovered the unreturned affection she bore him, which excited her Pity & Compassion so strongly that she addressed her in the following Manner.

"I perceive but too plainly my dear Miss Johnson, that your Heart has not been able to withstand the fascinating Charms of this young Man & I pity you sincerely. Is it a first Love?"

"It is."

"I am still more greived to hear *that;* I am myself a sad example of the Miseries, in general attendant on a first Love & I am determined for the future to avoid the like Misfortune. I wish it may not be too late for you to do the same; if it is not endeavour my dear Girl to secure yourself from so great a Danger. A second attachment is seldom attended with any serious consequences; against *that* therefore I have nothing to say. Preserve yourself from a first Love & you need not fear a second."

"You mentioned Madam something of your having yourself been a sufferer by the misfortune you are so good as to wish me to avoid. Will you favour me with your Life & Adventures?"

"Willingly my Love."

CHAPTER THE THIRD

"My Father was a gentleman of considerable Fortune in Berkshire; myself & a few more his only Children. I was but six years old when I had the misfortune of losing my Mother & being at that time young & Tender, my father instead of sending me to School, procured an able handed Governess to superintend my Education at Home. My Brothers were placed at Schools suitable to their Ages & my Sisters being all younger than myself, remained still under the Care of their Nurse.

Miss Dickins was an excellent Governess. She instructed me in the Paths of Virtue; under her tuition I daily became more amiable, & might perhaps by this time have nearly attained perfection, had not my worthy Preceptoress been torn from my arms, e'er I had attained my seventeenth year. I never shall forget her last words. 'My dear Kitty she said, Good night t'ye.' I never saw her afterwards" continued Lady Williams wiping her eyes, "She eloped with the Butler the same night."

"I was invited the following year by a distant relation of my Father's to spend the Winter with her in town. Mrs Watkins was a Lady of Fashion, Family & fortune; she was in general esteemed a pretty Woman, but I never thought her very handsome, for my part. She had too high a forehead, Her eyes were too small & she had too much colour."

"How can *that* be?" interrupted Miss Johnson reddening with anger; "Do you think that any one can have too much colour?"

"Indeed I do, & I'll tell you why I do my dear Alice; when a person has too great a degree of red in their Complexion, it gives their face in my opinion, too red a look."

"But can a face my Lady have too red a look?"

"Certainly my dear Miss Johnson & I'll [tell] you why. When a face has too red a look it does not appear to so much advantage as it would were it paler."

"Pray Ma'am proceed in your story."

"Well, as I said before, I was invited by this Lady to spend some weeks with her in town. Many Gentlemen thought her Handsome but in my opinion, Her forehead was too high, her eyes too small & she had too much colour."

"In that Madam as I said before your Ladyship must have been mistaken. Mrs. Watkins could not have too much colour since no one can have too much."

"Excuse me my Love if I do not agree with you in that particular. Let me explain myself clearly; my idea of the case is this. When a Woman has too great a proportion of red in her Cheeks, she must have too much colour."

"But Madam I deny that it is possible for any one to have too great a proportion of red in their Cheeks."

"What my Love not if they have too much colour?"

Miss Johnson was now out of all patience, the more so perhaps as Lady Williams still remained so inflexibly cool. It must be remembered however that her Ladyship had in one respect by far the advantage of Alice; I mean in not being drunk, for heated with wine & raised by Passion, she could have little command of her Temper.

The Dispute at length grew so hot on the part of Alice that, "From Words she almost came to Blows" When Mr Johnson luckily entered & with some difficulty forced her away from Lady Williams, Mrs Watkins & her red cheeks.

CHAPTER THE FOURTH

My Readers may perhaps imagine that after such a fracas, no intimacy could longer subsist between the Johnsons and Lady Williams, but in that they are mistaken for her Ladyship was too sensible to be angry at a conduct which she could not help perceiving to be the natural consequence of inebriety & Alice had too sincere a respect for Lady Williams & too great a relish for her Claret, not to make every concession in her power.

A few days after their reconciliation Lady Williams called on Miss Johnson to propose a walk in a Citron Grove which led from her Ladyship's pigstye to Charles Adams's Horsepond. Alice was too sensible of Lady Williams's kindness in proposing such a walk & too much pleased with the prospect of seeing at the end of it, a Horsepond of Charles's, not to accept it with visible delight. They had not proceeded far before she was roused from the reflection of the happiness she was going to enjoy, by Lady Williams's thus addressing her.

"I have as yet forborn my dear Alice to continue the narrative of my Life from an unwillingness of recalling to your Memory a scene which (since it reflects on you rather disgrace than credit) had better be forgot than remembered."

Alice had already begun to colour up & was beginning to speak, when her Ladyship perceiving her displeasure, continued thus.

"I am afraid my dear Girl that I have offended you by what I have just said; I assure you I do not mean to distress you by a retrospection of what cannot now be helped;

considering all things I do not think you so much to blame as many People do; for when a person is in Liquor, there is no answering for what they may do. [a woman (?) in such a situation is particularly off her guard because her head is not strong enough to support intoxication."][2]

"Madam, this is not to be borne; I insist—"

"My dear Girl dont vex yourself about the matter; I assure you I have entirely forgiven every thing respecting it; indeed I was not angry at the time, because as I saw all along, you were nearly dead drunk. I knew you could not help saying the strange things you did. But I see I distress you; so I will change the subject & desire it may never again be mentioned; remember it is all forgot—I will now pursue my story; but I must insist upon not giving you any description of Mrs Watkins; it would only be reviving old stories & as you never saw her, it can be nothing to you, if her forehead *was* too high, her eyes *were* too small, or if she *had* too much colour."

"Again! Lady Williams: this is too much"——

So provoked was poor Alice at this renewal of the old story, that I know not what might have been the consequence of it, had not their attention been engaged by another object. A lovely young Woman lying apparently in great pain beneath a Citron-tree, was an object too interesting not to attract their notice. Forgetting their own dispute they both with simpathizing tenderness advanced towards her & accosted her in these terms.

"You seem fair Nymph to be labouring under some misfortune which we shall be happy to releive if you will inform us what it is. Will you favour us with your Life & adventures?"

"Willingly Ladies, if you will be so kind as to be seated." They took their places & she thus began.

CHAPTER THE FIFTH

"I am a native of North Wales & my Father is one of the most capital Taylors in it. Having a numerous family, he was easily prevailed on by a sister of my Mother's who is a widow in good circumstances & keeps an alehouse in the next Village to ours, to let her take me & breed me up at her own expence. Accordingly I have lived with her for the last 8 years of my Life, during which time she provided me with some of the first rate Masters, who taught me all the accomplishments requisite for one of my sex and rank. Under their instructions I learned Dancing, Music, Drawing & various Languages, by which means I became more accomplished than any other Taylor's Daughter in Wales. Never was there a happier creature than I was, till within the last half year—but I should have told you before that the principal Estate in our Neighbourhood belongs to Charles Adams, the owner of the brick House, you see yonder."

"Charles Adams!" exclaimed the astonished Alice; "are you acquainted with Charles Adams?"

---

[2] Erased in MS.

"To my sorrow madam I am. He came about half a year ago to receive the rents of the Estate I have just mentioned. At that time I first saw him; as you seem ma'am acquainted with him, I need not describe to you how charming he is. I could not resist his attractions;"——

"Ah! who can," said Alice with a deep sigh.

"My aunt being in terms of the greatest intimacy with his cook, determined, at my request, to try whether she could discover, by means of her freind if there were any chance of his returning my affection. For this purpose she went one evening to drink tea with Mrs Susan, who in the course of Conversation mentioned the goodness of her Place & the Goodness of her Master; upon which my Aunt began pumping her with so much dexterity that in a short time Susan owned, that she did not think her Master would ever marry, 'for (said she) he has often & often declared to me that his wife, whoever she might be, must possess, Youth, Beauty, Birth, Wit, Merit, & Money. I have many a time (she continued) endeavoured to reason him out of his resolution & to convince him of the improbability of his ever meeting with such a Lady; but my arguments have had no effect & he continues as firm in his determination as ever.' You may imagine Ladies my distress on hearing this; for I was fearfull that tho' possessed of Youth, Beauty, Wit & Merit, & tho' the probable Heiress of my Aunts House & business, he might think me deficient in Rank, & in being so, unworthy of his hand."

"However I was determined to make a bold push & therefore wrote him a very kind letter, offering him with great tenderness my hand & heart. To this I received an angry & peremptory refusal, but thinking it might be rather the effect of his modesty than any thing else, I pressed him again on the subject. But he never answered any more of my Letters & very soon afterwards left the Country. As soon as I heard of his departure I wrote to him here, informing him that I should shortly do myself the honour of waiting on him at Pammydiddle, to which I received no answer; therefore choosing to take, Silence for Consent, I left Wales, unknown to my Aunt, & arrived here after a tedious Journey this Morning. On enquiring for his House I was directed thro' this Wood, to the one you there see. With a heart elated by the expected happiness of beholding him I entered it & had proceeded thus far in my progress thro' it, when I found myself suddenly seized by the leg & on examining the cause of it, found that I was caught in one of the steel traps so common in gentlemen's grounds."

"Ah cried Lady Williams, how fortunate we are to meet with you; since we might otherwise perhaps have shared the like misfortune"——

"It is indeed happy for you Ladies, that I should have been a short time before you. I screamed as you may easily imagine till the woods resounded again & till one of the inhuman Wretch's servants came to my assistance & released me from my dreadfull prison, but not before one of my legs was entirely broken."

CHAPTER THE SIXTH

At this melancholy recital the fair eyes of Lady Williams, were suffused in tears & Alice could not help exclaiming,

"Oh! cruel Charles to wound the hearts & legs of all the fair."

Lady Williams now interposed & observed that the young Lady's leg ought to be set without farther delay. After examining the fracture therefore, she immediately began & performed the operation with great skill which was the more wonderfull on account of her having never performed such a one before. Lucy, then arose from the ground & finding that she could walk with the greatest ease, accompanied them to Lady Williams's House at her Ladyship's particular request.

The perfect form, the beautifull face, & elegant manners of Lucy so won on the affections of Alice that when they parted, which was not till after Supper, she assured her that except her Father, Brother, Uncles, Aunts, Cousins & other relations, Lady Williams, Charles Adams & a few dozen more of particular freinds, she loved her better than almost any other person in the world.

Such a flattering assurance of her regard would justly have given much pleasure to the object of it, had she not plainly perceived that the amiable Alice had partaken too freely of Lady Williams's claret.

Her Ladyship (whose discernment was great) read in the intelligent countenance of Lucy her thoughts on the subject & as soon as Miss Johnson had taken her leave, thus addressed her.

"When you are more intimately acquainted with my Alice you will not be surprised, Lucy, to see the dear Creature drink a little too much; for such things happen every day. She has many rare & charming qualities, but Sobriety is not one of them. The whole Family are indeed a sad drunken set. I am sorry to say too that I never knew three such thorough Gamesters as they are, more particularly Alice. But she is a charming girl. I fancy not one of the sweetest tempers in the world; to be sure I have seen her in such passions! However she is a sweet young Woman. I am sure you'll like her. I scarcely know any one so amiable.—Oh! that you could but have seen her the other Evening! How she raved! & on such a trifle too! She is indeed a most pleasing Girl! I shall always love her!"

"She appears by your ladyship's account to have many good qualities", replied Lucy. "Oh! a thousand," answered Lady Williams; tho' I am very partial to her, and perhaps am blinded by my affection, to her real defects."

CHAPTER THE SEVENTH

The next morning brought the three Miss Simpsons to wait on Lady Williams, who received them with the utmost politeness & introduced to their acquaintance Lucy, with whom the eldest was so much pleased that at parting she declared her sole *ambi-*

tion was to have her accompany them the next morning to Bath, whither they were going for some weeks.

"Lucy, said Lady Williams, is quite at her own disposal & if she chooses to accept so kind an invitation, I hope she will not hesitate, from any motives of delicacy on my account. I know not indeed how I shall ever be able to part with her. She never was at Bath & I should think that it would be a most agreable Jaunt to her. Speak my Love, continued she, turning to Lucy, what say you to accompanying these Ladies? I shall be miserable without you—t'will be a most pleasant tour to you—I hope you'll go; if you do I am sure t'will be the Death of me—pray be persuaded"——

Lucy begged leave to decline the honour of accompanying them, with many expressions of gratitude for the extream politeness of Miss Simpson in inviting her.

Miss Simpson appeared much disappointed by her refusal. Lady Williams insisted on her going—declared that she would never forgive her if she did not, and that she should never survive it if she did, & inshort used such persuasive arguments that it was at length resolved she was to go. The Miss Simpsons called for her at ten o'clock the next morning & Lady Williams had soon the satisfaction of receiving from her young freind, the pleasing intelligence of their safe arrival in Bath.

It may now be proper to return to the Hero of this Novel, the brother of Alice, of whom I beleive I have scarcely ever had occasion to speak; which may perhaps be partly oweing to his unfortunate propensity to Liquor, which so compleatly deprived him of the use of those faculties Nature had endowed him with, that he never did anything worth mentioning. His Death happened a short time after Lucy's departure & was the natural Consequence of this pernicious practice. By his decease, his sister became the sole inheritress of a very large fortune, which as it gave her fresh Hopes of rendering herself acceptable as a wife to Charles Adams could not fail of being most pleasing to her—& as the effect was Joyfull the Cause could scarcely be lamented.

Finding the violence of her attachment to him daily augment, she at length disclosed it to her Father & desired him to propose a union between them to Charles. Her father consented & set out one morning to open the affair to the young Man. Mr Johnson being a man of few words his part was soon performed & the answer he received was as follows—

"Sir, I may perhaps be expected to appeared [*sic*] pleased at & gratefull for the offer you have made me: but let me tell you that I consider it as an affront. I look upon myself to be Sir a perfect Beauty—where would you see a finer figure or a more charming face. Then, sir I imagine my Manners & Address to be of the most polished kind; there is a certain elegance a peculiar sweetness in them that I never saw equalled & cannot describe—. Partiality aside, I am certainly more accomplished in every Language, every Science, every Art and every thing than any other person in Europe. My temper is even, my virtues innumerable, my self unparalelled. Since such Sir is my character, what do you mean by wishing me to marry your Daughter? Let me give you a short sketch of yourself & of her. I look upon you Sir to be a very good sort of Man in the main; a drunken old Dog to be sure, but that's nothing to me. Your daughter sir, is neither sufficiently beautifull, sufficiently amiable, sufficiently witty, nor sufficiently rich for me—. I expect nothing more in my wife than my wife will find in me—Perfection. These sir, are my sentiments & I honour myself for having such. One freind I have & glory in having but one—. She is at present preparing my Dinner, but if you choose to see her, she shall come & she will inform you that these have ever been my sentiments."

Mr Johnson was satisfied: & expressing himself to be much obliged to Mr Adams for the characters he had favoured him with of himself & his Daughter, took his leave.

The unfortunate Alice on receiving from her father the sad account of the ill success his visit had been attended with, could scarcely support the disappointment—She flew to her Bottle & it was soon forgot.

CHAPTER THE EIGHTH

While these affairs were transacting at Pammydiddle, Lucy was conquering ever [sic] Heart at Bath. A fortnight's residence there had nearly effaced from her remembrance the captivating form of Charles—The recollection of what her Heart had formerly suffered by his charms & her Leg by his trap, enabled her to forget him with tolerable Ease, which was what she determined to do; & for that purpose dedicated five minutes in every day to the employment of driving him from her remembrance.

Her second Letter to Lady Williams contained the pleasing intelligence of her having accomplished her undertaking to her entire satisfaction; she mentioned in it also an offer of marriage she had received from the Duke of ——— an elderly Man of noble fortune whose ill health was the chief inducement of his Journey to Bath. "I am distressed (she continued) to know whether I mean to accept him or not. There are a thousand advantages to be derived from a marriage with the Duke, for besides those more inferior ones of Rank & Fortune it will procure me a home, which of all other things is what I most desire. Your Ladyship's kind wish of my always remaining with you, is noble & generous but I cannot think of becoming so great a burden on one I so much love & esteem. That one should receive obligations only from those we despise, is a sentiment instilled into my mind by my worthy aunt, in my early years, & cannot in my opinion be too strictly adhered to. The excellent woman of whom I now speak, is I hear too much incensed by my imprudent departure from Wales, to receive me again—. I most earnestly wish to leave the Ladies I am now with. Miss Simpson is indeed (setting aside ambition) very amiable, but her 2d Sister the envious & malvolent Sukey is too disagreable to live with. I have reason to think that the admiration I have met with in the circles of the Great at this Place, has raised her Hatred & Envy; for often has she threatened, & sometimes endeavoured to cut my throat.—Your Ladyship will therefore allow that I am not wrong in wishing to leave Bath, & in wishing to have a home to receive me, when I do. I shall expect with impatience your advice concerning the Duke & am your most obliged

&c. LUCY."

Lady Williams sent her, her opinion on the subject in the following Manner.

"Why do you hesitate my dearest Lucy, a moment with respect to the Duke? I have enquired into his Character & find him to be an unprincipaled, illiterate Man. Never shall my Lucy be united to such a one! He has a princely fortune, which is every day encreasing. How nobly will you spend it!, what credit will you give him in the eyes of all!, How much will he be respected on his Wife's account! But why my dearest Lucy, why will you not at once decide this affair by returning to me & never leaving me again? Altho' I admire your noble sentiments with respect to obligations, yet, let me beg that they may not prevent your making me happy. It will to be sure be a great expence to me, to have you always with me—I shall not be able to support it—but what is that in comparison with the happiness I shall enjoy in your society?—'twill ruin me I know—you will not therefore surely, withstand these arguments, or refuse to return to yours most affectionately &c. &c.

C. WILLIAMS"

CHAPTER THE NINTH

What might have been the effect of her Ladyship's advice, had it ever been received by Lucy, is uncertain, as it reached Bath a few Hours after she had breathed her last. She fell a sacrifice to the Envy & Malice of Sukey who jealous of her superior charms took her by poison from an admiring World at the age of seventeen.

Thus fell the amiable & lovely Lucy whose Life had been marked by no crime, and stained by no blemish but her imprudent departure from her Aunts, & whose death was sincerely lamented by every one who knew her. Among the most afflicted of her freinds were Lady Williams, Miss Johnson & the Duke; the 2 first of whom had a most sincere regard for her, more particularly Alice, who had spent a whole evening in her company & had never thought of her since. His Grace's affliction may likewise be easily accounted for, since he lost one for whom he had experienced during the last ten days, a tender affection & sincere regard. He mourned her loss with unshaken constancy for the next fortnight at the end of which time, he gratified the ambition of Caroline Simpson by raising her to the rank of a Dutchess. Thus was she at length rendered compleatly happy in the gratification of her favourite passion. Her sister the perfidious Sukey, was likewise shortly after exalted in a manner she truly deserved, & by her actions appeared to have always desired. Her barbarous Murder was discovered & in spite of every interceding freind she was speedily raised to the Gallows—. The beautifull but affected Cecilia was too sensible of her own superior charms, not to imagine that if Caroline could engage a Duke, she might without censure aspire to the affections of some Prince—& knowing that those of her native Country were cheifly engaged, she left England & I have since heard is at present the favourite Sultana of the great Mogul—.

In the mean time the inhabitants of Pammydiddle were in a state of the greatest astonishment & Wonder, a report being circulated of the intended marriage of Charles Adams. The Lady's name was still a secret. Mr & Mrs Jones imagined it to be, Miss Johnson; but *she* knew better; all *her* fears were centered in his Cook, when to the astonishment of every one, he was publicly united to Lady Williams—

FINIS

Edgar & Emma

A Tale

CHAPTER THE FIRST

"I cannot imagine," said Sir Godfrey to his Lady, "why we continue in such deplorable Lodgings as these, in a paltry Market-town, while we have 3 good Houses of our own situated in some of the finest parts of England, & perfectly ready to receive us!"

"I'm sure Sir Godfrey," replied Lady Marlow, "it has been much against my inclination that we have staid here so long; or why we should ever have come at all indeed, has been to me a wonder, as none of our Houses have been in the least want of repair."

"Nay my dear," answered Sir Godfrey, "you are the last person who ought to be displeased with what was always meant as a compliment to you; for you cannot but be sensible of the very great inconvenience your Daughters & I have been put to, during the 2 years we have remained crowded in these Lodgings in order to give you pleasure."

"My dear," replied Lady Marlow, "How can you stand & tell such lies, when you very well know that it was merely to oblige the Girls & you, that I left a most commodious House situated in a most delightfull Country & surrounded by a most agreable Neighbourhood, to live 2 years cramped up in Lodgings three pair of stairs high, in a smokey & unwholesome town, which has given me a continual fever & almost thrown me into a Consumption."

As, after a few more speeches on both sides, they could not determine which was the most to blame, they prudently laid aside the debate, & having packed up their Cloathes & paid their rent, they set out the next morning with their 2 Daughters for their seat in Sussex.

Sir Godfrey & Lady Marlow were indeed very sensible people & tho' (as in this instance) like many other sensible People, they sometimes did a foolish thing, yet in general their actions were guided by Prudence & regulated by discretion.

After a Journey of two Days & a half they arrived at Marlhurst in good health & high spirits; so overjoyed were they all to inhabit again a place, they had left with mutual regret for two years, that they ordered the bells to be rung & distributed ninepence among the Ringers.

CHAPTER THE SECOND

The news of their arrival being quickly spread throughout the Country, brought them in a few Days visits of congratulation from every family in it.

Amongst the rest came the inhabitants of Willmot Lodge a beautifull Villa not far from Marlhurst. Mr Willmot was the representative of a very ancient Family & possessed besides his paternal Estate, a considerable share in a Lead mine & a ticket in the Lottery. His Lady was an agreable Woman. Their Children were too numerous to be particularly described; it is sufficient to say that in general they were virtuously inclined & not given to any wicked ways. Their family being too large to accompany them in every visit, they took nine with them alternately. When their Coach stopped at Sir Godfrey's door, the Miss Marlow's Hearts throbbed in the eager expectation of once more beholding a family so dear to them. Emma the youngest (who was more particularly interested in their arrival, being attached to their eldest Son) continued at her Dressing-room window in anxious Hopes of seeing young Edgar descend from the Carriage.

Mr & Mrs Willmot with their three eldest Daughters first appeared—Emma began to tremble. Robert, Richard, Ralph, & Rodolphus followed—Emma turned pale. Their two youngest Girls were lifted from the Coach—Emma sunk breathless on a Sopha. A footman came to announce to her the arrival of Company; her heart was too full to contain its afflictions. A confidante was necessary—In Thomas she hoped to experience a faithfull one—for one she must have & Thomas was the only one at Hand. To him she unbosomed herself without restraint & after owning her passion for young Willmot, requested his advice in what manner she should conduct herself in the melancholy Disappointment under which she laboured.

Thomas, who would gladly have been excused from listening to her complaint, begged leave to decline giving any advice concerning it, which much against her will, she was obliged to comply with.

Having dispatched him therefore with many injunctions of secrecy, she descended with a heavy heart into the Parlour, where she found the good Party seated in a social Manner round a blazing fire.

CHAPTER THE THIRD

Emma had continued in the Parlour some time before she could summon up sufficient courage to ask Mrs Willmot after the rest of her family; & when she did, it was in so low, so faltering a voice that no one knew she spoke. Dejected by the ill success of her first attempt she made no other, till on Mrs Willmots desiring one of the little Girls to ring the bell for their Carriage, she stepped across the room & seizing the string said in a resolute manner.

"Mrs Willmot, you do not stir from this House till you let me know how all the rest of your family do, particularly your eldest son.'

They were all greatly surprised by such an unexpected address & the more so, on account of the manner in which it was spoken; but Emma, who would not be again disappointed, requesting an answer, Mrs Willmot made the following eloquent oration.

"Our children are all extremely well but at present most of them from home. Amy is with my sister Clayton. Sam at Eton. David with his Uncle John. Jem & Will at Winchester. Kitty at Queen's Square. Ned with his Grandmother. Hetty & Patty in a Convent at Brussells. Edgar at college, Peter at Nurse, & all the rest (except the nine here) at home."

It was with difficulty that Emma could refrain from tears on hearing of the absence of Edgar; she remained however tolerably composed till the Willmot's were gone when having no check to the overflowings of her greif, she gave free vent to them, & retiring to her own room, continued in tears the remainder of her Life.

FINIS

Henry and Eliza

A Novel

Is humbly dedicated to Miss Cooper by her obedient Humble Servant

THE AUTHOR

As Sir George and Lady Harcourt were superintending the Labours of their Haymakers, rewarding the industry of some by smiles of approbation, & punishing the idleness of others, by a cudgel, they perceived lying closely concealed beneath the thick foliage of a Haycock, a beautifull little Girl not more than 3 months old.

Touched with the enchanting Graces of her face & delighted with the infantine tho'
sprightly answers she returned to their many questions, they resolved to take her home &,
having no Children of their own, to educate her with care & cost.

Being good People themselves, their first & principal care was to incite in her a Love
of Virtue & a Hatred of Vice, in which they so well succeeded (Eliza having a natural
turn that way herself) that when she grew up, she was the delight of all who knew her.

Beloved by Lady Harcourt, adored by Sir George & admired by all the World, she
lived in a continued course of uninterrupted Happiness, till she had attained her eighteenth year, when happening one day to be detected in stealing a banknote of 50£, she
was turned out of doors by her inhuman Benefactors. Such a transition to one who did
not possess so noble & exalted a mind as Eliza, would have been Death, but she, happy
in the conscious knowledge of her own Excellence, amused herself, as she sate beneath
a tree with making & singing the following Lines.

SONG

Though misfortunes my footsteps may ever attend
   I hope I shall never have need of a Freind
as an innocent Heart I will ever preserve
   and will never from Virtue's dear boundaries swerve.

Having amused herself some hours, with this song & her own pleasing reflections,
she arose & took the road to M. a small market town of which place her most intimate
freind kept the red Lion.

To this freind she immediately went, to whom having recounted her late misfortune, she communicated her wish of getting into some family in the capacity of Humble Companion.

Mrs Willson, who was the most amiable creature on earth, was no sooner acquainted
with her Desire, than she sate down in the Bar & wrote the following Letter to the
Dutchess of F, the woman whom of all others, she most Esteemed.

"TO THE DUTCHESS OF F."

Receive into your Family, at my request a young woman of unexceptionable Character, who is so good as to choose your Society in preference to going to Service. Hasten,
& take her from the arms of your

SARAH WILSON."

The Dutchess, whose freindship for Mrs Wilson would have carried her any lengths,
was overjoyed at such an opportunity of obliging her & accordingly sate out immediately on the receipt of her letter for the red Lion, which she reached the same Evening.

The Dutchess of F. was about 45 & a half; Her passions were strong, her freindships firm & her Enmities, unconquerable. She was a widow & had only one Daughter who was on the point of marriage with a young Man of considerable fortune.

The Dutchess no sooner beheld our Heroine than throwing her arms around her neck, she declared herself so much pleased with her, that she was resolved they never more should part. Eliza was delighted with such a protestation of freindship, & after taking a most affecting leave of her dear Mrs Wilson, accompanied her grace the next morning to her seat in Surry.

With every expression of regard did the Dutchess introduce her to Lady Hariet, who was so much pleased with her appearance that she besought her, to consider her as her Sister, which Eliza with the greatest Condescension promised to do.

Mr Cecil, the Lover of Lady Harriet, being often with the family was often with Eliza. A mutual Love took place & Cecil having declared his first, prevailed on Eliza to consent to a private union, which was easy to be effected, as the dutchess's chaplain being very much in love with Eliza himself, would they were certain do anything to oblige her.

The Dutchess & Lady Harriet being engaged one evening to an assembly, they took the opportunity of their absence & were united by the enamoured Chaplain.

When the Ladies returned, their amazement was great at finding instead of Eliza the following Note.

"MADAM

We are married & gone.

HENRY & ELIZA CECIL."

Her Grace as soon as she had read the letter, which sufficiently explained the whole affair, flew into the most violent passion & after having spent an agreable half hour, in calling them by all the shocking Names her rage could suggest to her, sent out after them 300 armed Men, with orders not to return without their Bodies, dead or alive; intending that if they should be brought to her in the latter condition to have them put to Death in some torturelike manner, after a few years Confinement.

In the mean time Cecil & Eliza continued their flight to the Continent, which they judged to be more secure than their native Land, from the dreadfull effects of the Dutchess's vengeance, which they had so much reason to apprehend.

In France they remained 3 years, during which time they became the parents of two Boys, & at the end of it Eliza became a widow without any thing to support either her or her Children. They had lived since their Marriage at the rate of 18,000£ a year, of which Mr Cecil's estate being rather less than the twentieth part, they had been able to save but a trifle, having lived to the utmost extent of their Income.

Eliza, being perfectly conscious of the derangement in their affairs, immediately on her Husband's death set sail for England, in a man of War of 55 Guns, which they had built in their more prosperous Days. But no sooner had she stepped on Shore at

Dover, with a Child in each hand, than she was seized by the officers of the Dutchess, & conducted by them to a snug little Newgate of their Lady's, which she had erected for the reception of her own private Prisoners.

No sooner had Eliza entered her Dungeon than the first thought which occurred to her, was how to get out of it again.

She went to the Door; but it was locked. She looked at the Window; but it was barred with iron; disappointed in both her expectations, she dispaired of effecting her Escape, when she fortunately perceived in a Corner of her Cell, a small saw & Ladder of ropes. With the saw she instantly went to work & in a few weeks had displaced every Bar but one to which she fastened the Ladder.

A difficulty then occurred which for some time, she knew not how to obviate. Her Children were too small to get down the Ladder by themselves, nor would it be possible for her to take them in her arms, when *she* did. At last she determined to fling down all her Cloathes, of which she had a large Quantity, & then having given them strict Charge not to hurt themselves, threw her Children after them. She herself with ease discended by the Ladder, at the bottom of which she had the pleasure of finding her little boys in perfect Health & fast asleep.

Her wardrobe she now saw a fatal necessity of selling, both for the preservation of her Children & herself. With tears in her eyes, she parted with these last reliques of her former Glory, & with the money she got for them, bought others more usefull, some playthings for Her Boys and a gold Watch for herself.

But scarcely was she provided with the above-mentioned necessaries, than she began to find herself rather hungry, & had reason to think, by their biting off two of her fingers, that her Children were much in the same situation.

To remedy these unavoidable misfortunes, she determined to return to her old freinds, Sir George & Lady Harcourt, whose generosity she had so often experienced & hoped to experience as often again.

She had about 40 miles to travel before she could reach their hospitable Mansion, of which having walked 30 without stopping, she found herself at the Entrance of a Town, where often in happier times, she had accompanied Sir George & Lady Harcourt to regale themselves with a cold collation at one of the Inns.

The reflections that her adventures since the last time she had partaken of these happy *Junketings,* afforded her, occupied her mind, for some time, as she sate on the steps at the door of a Gentleman's house. As soon as these reflections were ended, she arose & determined to take her station at the very inn, she remembered with so much delight, from the Company of which, as they went in & out, she hoped to receive some Charitable Gratuity.

She had but just taken her post at the Innyard before a Carriage drove out of it, & on turning the Corner at which she was stationed, stopped to give the Postilion an opportunity of admiring the beauty of the prospect. Eliza then advanced to the carriage & was going to request their Charity, when on fixing her Eyes on the Lady, within it, she exclaimed,

"Lady Harcourt!"

To which the lady replied,

"Eliza!"

"Yes Madam it is the wretched Eliza herself."

Sir George, who was also in the Carriage, but too much amazed to speek, was proceeding to demand an explanation from Eliza of the Situation she was then in, when Lady Harcourt in transports of Joy, exclaimed.

"Sir George, Sir George, she is not only Eliza our adopted Daughter, but our real Child."

"Our real Child! What Lady Harcourt, do you mean? You know you never even was with child. Explain yourself, I beseech you."

"You must remember Sir George, that when you sailed for America, you left me breeding."

"I do, I do, go on dear Polly."

"Four months after you were gone, I was delivered of this Girl, but dreading your just resentment at her not proving the Boy you wished, I took her to a Haycock & laid her down. A few weeks afterwards, you returned, & fortunately for me, made no enquiries on the subject. Satisfied within myself of the wellfare of my Child, I soon forgot I had one, insomuch that when, we shortly after found her in the very Haycock, I had placed her, I had no more idea of her being my own, than you had, & nothing I will venture to say would have recalled the circumstance to my remembrance, but my thus accidentally hearing her voice, which now strikes me as being the very counterpart of my own Child's."

"The rational & convincing Account you have given of the whole affair, said Sir George, leaves no doubt of her being our Daughter & as such I freely forgive the robbery she was guilty of."

A mutual Reconciliation then took place, & Eliza, ascending the Carriage with her two Children returned to that home from which she had been absent nearly four years.

No sooner was she reinstated in her accustomed power at Harcourt Hall, than she raised an Army, with which she entirely demolished the Dutchess's Newgate, snug as it was, and by that act, gained the Blessings of thousands, & the Applause of her own Heart.

FINIS

The Adventures of Mr Harley

a short, but interesting Tale, is with all imaginable Respect inscribed to Mr Francis William Austen Midshipman on board his Majestys Ship the Perseverance by his Obedient Servant

THE AUTHOR.

Mr Harley was one of many Children. Destined by his father for the Church & by his Mother for the Sea, desirous of pleasing both, he prevailed on Sir John to obtain for him a Chaplaincy on board a Man of War. He accordingly, cut his Hair and sailed.

In half a year he returned & set-off in the Stage Coach for Hogsworth Green, the seat of Emma. His fellow travellers were, A man without a Hat, Another with two, An old maid & a young Wife.

This last appeared about 17 with fine dark Eyes & an elegant Shape; inshort Mr Harley soon found out, that she was his Emma & recollected he had married her a few weeks before he left England.

FINIS

Sir William Mountague

an unfinished performance
is humbly dedicated to Charles John
Austen Esqre, by his most obedient humble
Servant

THE AUTHOR

Sir William Mountague was the son of Sir Henry Mountague, who was the son of Sir John Mountague, a descendant of Sir Christopher Mountague, who was the nephew of Sir Edward Mountague, whose ancestor was Sir James Mountague a near relation of Sir Robert Mountague, who inherited the Title & Estate from Sir Frederic Mountague.

Sir William was about 17 when his Father died, & left him a handsome fortune, an ancient House & a Park well stocked with Deer. Sir William had not been long in the possession of his Estate before he fell in Love with the 3 Miss Cliftons of Kilhoobery Park. These young Ladies were all equally young, equally handsome, equally rich & equally amiable—Sir William was equally in Love with them all, & knowing not which to prefer, he left the Country & took Lodgings in a small Village near Dover.

In this retreat, to which he had retired in the hope of finding a shelter from the Pangs of Love, he became enamoured of a young Widow of Quality, who came for change of air to the same Village, after the death of a Husband, whom she had always tenderly loved & now sincerely lamented.

Lady Percival was young, accomplished & lovely. Sir William adored her & she consented to become his Wife. Vehemently pressed by Sir William to name the Day in which he might conduct her to the Altar, she at length fixed on the following Monday, which was the first of September. Sir William was a Shot & could not support the idea of losing such a Day, even for such a Cause. He begged her to delay the Wedding a short time. Lady Percival was enraged & returned to London the next Morning.

Sir William was sorry to lose her, but as he knew that he should have been much more greived by the Loss of the 1st of September, his Sorrow was not without a mixture of Happiness, & his Affliction was considerably lessened by his Joy.

After staying at the Village a few weeks longer, he left it & went to a freind's House in Surry. Mr Brudenell was a sensible Man, & had a beautifull Neice with whom Sir William soon fell in love. But Miss Arundel was cruel; she preferred a Mr Stanhope: Sir William shot Mr Stanhope; the lady had then no reason to refuse him; she accepted him, & they were to be married on the 27th of October. But on the 25th Sir William received a visit from Emma Stanhope the sister of the unfortunate Victim of his rage. She begged some recompence, some atonement for the cruel Murder of her Brother. Sir William bade her name her price. She fixed on S/14. Sir William offered her himself & Fortune. They went to London the next day & were there privately married. For a fortnight Sir William was compleatly happy, but chancing one day to see a charming young Woman entering a Chariot in Brook Street, he became again most violently in love. On enquiring the name of this fair Unknown, he found that she was the Sister of his old freind Lady Percival, at which he was much rejoiced, as he hoped to have, by his acquaintance with her Ladyship, free access to Miss Wentworth. . . . .

FINIS

To Charles John Austen Esqre

S<small>IR</small>,

Your generous patronage of the unfinished tale, I have already taken the Liberty of dedicating to you, encourages me to dedicate to you a second, as unfinished as the first.

I am Sir with every expression

of regard for you & yr noble

Family, your most obedt

&c. &c. . . .

T<small>HE</small> A<small>UTHOR</small>

Memoirs of Mr Clifford

An Unfinished Tale

Mr Clifford lived at Bath; & having never seen London, set off one monday morning determined to feast his eyes with a sight of that great Metropolis. He travelled in his Coach & Four, for he was a very rich young Man & kept a great many Carriages of which I do not recollect half. I can only remember that he had a Coach, a Chariot, a Chaise, a Landeau, a Landeaulet, a Phaeton, a Gig, a Whisky, an italian Chair, a Buggy, a Curricle & a wheelbarrow. He had likewise an amazing fine stud of Horses. To my knowledge he had six Greys, 4 Bays, eight Blacks & a poney.

In his Coach & 4 Bays Mr Clifford sate forward about 5 o'clock on Monday Morning the 1st of May for London. He always travelled remarkably expeditiously & contrived therefore to get to Devizes from Bath, which is no less than nineteen miles, the first Day. To be sure he did not get in till eleven at night & pretty tight work it was as you may imagine.

However when he was once got to Devizes he was determined to comfort himself with a good hot Supper and therefore ordered a whole Egg to be boiled for him & his Servants. The next morning he pursued his Journey & in the course of 3 days hard labour reached Overton, where he was seized with a dangerous fever the Consequence of too violent Exercise.

Five months did our Hero remain in this celebrated City under the care of its no less celebrated Physician, who at length compleatly cured him of his troublesome Desease.

As Mr Clifford still continued very weak, his first Day's Journey carried him only to Dean Gate, where he remained a few Days & found himself much benefited by the change of Air.

In easy Stages he proceeded to Basingstoke. One day Carrying him to Clarkengreen, the next to Worting, the 3d to the bottom of Basingstoke Hill, & the fourth, to Mr Robins's. . . .

FINIS

The Beautifull Cassandra

A Novel in Twelve Chapters

dedicated by permission to Miss Austen.
Dedication.

MADAM

You are a Phoenix. Your taste is refined, your Sentiments are noble, & your Virtues innumerable. Your Person is lovely, your Figure, elegant, & your Form, magestic. Your Manners are polished, your Conversation is rational & your appearance singular. If therefore the following Tale will afford one moment's amusement to you, every wish will be gratified of

Your most obedient
humble servant
THE AUTHOR

CHAPTER THE FIRST

Cassandra was the Daughter & the only Daughter of a celebrated Millener in Bond Street. Her father was of noble Birth, being the near relation of the Dutchess of ——'s Butler.

CHAPTER THE 2D

When Cassandra had attained her 16th year, she was lovely & amiable & chancing to fall in love with an elegant Bonnet, her Mother had just compleated bespoke by the Countess of —— she placed it on her gentle Head & walked from her Mother's shop to make her Fortune.

CHAPTER THE 3D

The first person she met, was the Viscount of —— a young Man, no less celebrated for his Accomplishments & Virtues, than for his Elegance & Beauty. She curtseyed & walked on.

CHAPTER THE 4TH

She then proceeded to a Pastry-cooks where she devoured six ices, refused to pay for them, knocked down the Pastry Cook & walked away.

CHAPTER THE 5TH

She next ascended a Hackney Coach & ordered it to Hampstead, where she was no sooner arrived than she ordered the Coachman to turn round & drive her back again.

CHAPTER THE 6TH

Being returned to the same spot of the same Street she had sate out from, the Coachman demanded his Pay.

CHAPTER THE 7TH

She searched her pockets over again & again; but every search was unsuccessfull. No money could she find. The man grew peremptory. She placed her bonnet on his head & ran away.

CHAPTER THE 8TH

Thro' many a street she then proceeded & met in none the least Adventure till on turning a Corner of Bloomsbury Square, she met Maria.

CHAPTER THE 9TH

Cassandra started & Maria seemed surprised; they trembled, blushed, turned pale & passed each other in a mutual silence.

CHAPTER THE 10TH

Cassandra was next accosted by her freind the Widow, who squeezing out her little Head thro' her less window, asked her how she did? Cassandra curtseyed & went on.

CHAPTER THE 11TH

A quarter of a mile brought her to her paternal roof in Bond Street from which she had now been absent nearly 7 hours.

CHAPTER THE 12TH

She entered it & was pressed to her Mother's bosom by that worthy Woman. Cassandra smiled & whispered to herself "This is a day well spent."

FINIS

Amelia Webster

an interesting & well written Tale
is dedicated by Permission
to
Mrs Austen
by
Her humble Servant

THE AUTHOR

Letter the first

TO MISS WEBSTER

MY DEAR AMELIA

You will rejoice to hear of the return of my amiable Brother from abroad. He arrived on thursday, & never did I see a finer form, save that of your sincere freind

MATILDA HERVEY

Letter the 2d

TO H. BEVERLEY ESQRE

DEAR BEVERLEY

I arrived here last thursday & met with a hearty reception from my Father, Mother & Sisters. The latter are both fine Girls—particularly Maud, who I think would suit you as a Wife well enough. What say you to this? She will have two thousand Pounds & as much more as you can get. If you don't marry her you will mortally offend

GEORGE HERVEY

Letter the 3d

TO MISS HERVEY

DEAR MAUD

Beleive me I'm happy to hear of your Brother's arrival. I have a thousand things to tell you, but my paper will only permit me to add that I am yr affect Freind

AMELIA WEBSTER

Letter the 4th

TO MISS S. HERVEY

DEAR SALLY

I have found a very convenient old hollow oak to put our Letters in; for you know we have long maintained a private Correspondence. It is about a mile from my House & seven from yours. You may perhaps imagine that I might have made choice of a tree which would have divided the Distance more equally—I was sensible of this at the time, but as I considered that the walk would be of benefit to you in your weak & uncertain state of Health, I preferred it to one nearer your House, & am yr faithfull

BENJAMIN BAR

Letter the 5th

TO MISS HERVEY

DEAR MAUD

I write now to inform you that I did not stop at your house in my way to Bath last Monday.—I have many things to inform you of besides; but my Paper reminds me of concluding; & beleive me yrs ever &c.

AMELIA WEBSTER

Letter the 6th

TO MISS WEBSTER

MADAM SATURDAY

An humble Admirer now addresses you.—I saw you lovely Fair one as you passed on Monday last, before our House in your way to Bath. I saw you thro' a telescope, & was so struck by your Charms that from that time to this I have not tasted human food.

GEORGE HERVEY

Letter the 7th

TO JACK

As I was this morning at Breakfast the Newspaper was brought me, & in the list of Marriages I read the following.

"George Hervey Esqre to Miss Amelia Webster"

"Henry Beverley Esqre to Miss Hervey"

&

"Benjamin Bar Esqre to Miss Sarah Hervey".

YOURS, TOM

FINIS

The Visit

A Comedy in 2 Acts

Dedication
To the Revd James Austen

SIR,

The following Drama, which I humbly recommend to your Protection & Patronage, tho' inferior to those celebrated Comedies called "The School for Jealousy" & "The travelled Man", will I hope afford some amusement to so respectable a *Curate* as yourself; which was the end in veiw when it was first composed by your Humble Servant the Author.

Dramatis Personae

Sir Arthur Hampton   Lady Hampton
Lord Fitzgerald   Miss Fitzgerald
Stanly   Sophy Hampton
Willoughby, Sir Arthur's nephew   Cloe Willoughby

The scenes are laid in Lord Fitzgerald's House.

Act the First

Scene the first, a Parlour——

enter LORD FITZGERALD & STANLY

STANLY. Cousin your servant.

FITZGERALD. Stanly, good morning to you. I hope you slept well last night.

STANLY. Remarkably well, I thank you.

FITZGERALD. I am afraid you found your Bed too short. It was bought in my Grand-mother's time, who was herself a very short woman & made a point of suiting all her Beds to her own length, as she never wished to have any company in the House, on account of an unfortunate impediment in her speech, which she was sensible of being very disagreable to her inmates.

STANLY. Make no more excuses dear Fitzgerald.

FITZGERALD. I will not distress you by too much civility—I only beg you will consider yourself as much at home as in your Father's house. Remember, "The more free, the more Wellcome."

[exit FITZGERALD

STANLY. Amiable Youth!
"Your virtues could he imitate
How happy would be Stanly's fate!"

[exit STANLY

Scene the 2d

STANLY & MISS FITZGERALD, *discovered.*

STANLY. What Company is it you expect to dine with you to Day, Cousin?

MISS F. Sir Arthur & Lady Hampton; their Daughter, Nephew & Neice.

STANLY. Miss Hampton & her Cousin are both Handsome, are they not?

MISS F. Miss Willoughby is extreamly so. Miss Hampton is a fine Girl, but not equal to her.

STANLY. Is not your Brother attached to the Latter?

MISS F. He admires her I know, but I beleive nothing more. Indeed I have heard him say that she was the most beautifull, pleasing, & amiable Girl in the world, & that of all others he should prefer her for his Wife. But it never went any farther I'm certain.

STANLY. And yet my Cousin never says a thing he does not mean.

MISS F. Never. From his Cradle he has always been a strict adherent to Truth [He never told a Lie but once, & that was merely to oblige me. Indeed I may truly say there never was such a Brother!]³

[Exeunt Severally

End of the First Act.

Act the Second

Scene the first. The Drawing Room.

Chairs set round in a row. LORD FITZGERALD, MISS FITZGERALD & STANLY *seated.*

Enter a Servant.

SERVANT. Sir Arthur & Lady Hampton. Miss Hampton, Mr & Miss Willoughby.

[exit SERVANT

Enter the Company.

MISS F. I hope I have the pleasure of seeing your Ladyship well. Sir Arthur, your servant. Yrs Mr Willoughby. Dear Sophy, Dear Cloe,—

[They pay their Compliments alternately.

MISS F. Pray be seated.

[They sit

Bless me! there ought to be 8 Chairs & there are but 6. However, if your Ladyship will but take Sir Arthur in your Lap, & Sophy my Brother in hers, I beleive we shall do pretty well.

LADY H. Oh! with pleasure....

SOPHY. I beg his Lordship would be seated.

MISS F. I am really shocked at crouding you in such a manner, but my Grandmother (who bought all the furniture of this room) as she had never a very large Party, did not think it necessary to buy more Chairs than were sufficient for her own family and two of her particular freinds.

---

³ Erased in MS.

SOPHY. I beg you will make no apologies. Your Brother is very light.

STANLY, *aside*) What a cherub is Cloe!

CLOE, *aside*) What a seraph is Stanly!

Enter a Servant.

SERVANT. Dinner is on table.

[*They all rise.*

MISS F. Lady Hampton, Miss Hampton, Miss Willoughby.

STANLY *hands* CLOE, LORD FITZGERALD, SOPHY, WILLOUGHBY, MISS FITZGERALD, *and* SIR ARTHUR, LADY HAMPTON.

[*Exeunt.*

Scene the 2d

The Dining Parlour.

MISS FITZGERALD *at top.* LORD FITZGERALD *at bottom. Company ranged on each side. Servants waiting.*

CLOE. I shall trouble Mr Stanly for a Little of the fried Cowheel & Onion.

STANLY. Oh Madam, there is a secret pleasure in helping so amiable a Lady—.

LADY H. I assure you my Lord, Sir Arthur never touches wine; but Sophy will toss off a bumper I am sure to oblige your Lordship.

LORD F. Elder wine or Mead, Miss Hampton?

SOPHY. If it is equal to you Sir, I should prefer some warm ale with a toast and nutmeg.

LORD F. Two glasses of warmed ale with a toast and nutmeg.

MISS F. I am afraid Mr Willoughby you take no care of yourself. I fear you dont meet with any thing to your liking.

WILLOUGHBY. Oh! Madam, I can want for nothing while there are red herrings on table.

LORD F. Sir Arthur taste that Tripe. I think you will not find it amiss.

LADY H. Sir Arthur never eats Tripe; tis too savoury for him you know my Lord.

MISS F. Take away the Liver & Crow & bring in the suet pudding.

(*a short Pause.*)

MISS F. Sir Arthur shant I send you a bit of pudding?

LADY H. Sir Arthur never eats suet pudding Ma'am. It is too high a Dish for him.

MISS F. Will no one allow me the honour of helping them? Then John take away the Pudding, & bring the Wine.

[SERVANTS *take away the things and bring in the Bottles & Glasses.*

LORD F. I wish we had any Desert to offer you. But my Grandmother in her Lifetime, destroyed the Hothouse in order to build a receptacle for the Turkies with it's materials; & we have never been able to raise another tolerable one.

LADY H. I beg you will make no apologies my Lord.

WILLOUGHBY. Come Girls, let us circulate the Bottle.

SOPHY. A very good notion Cousin; & I will second it with all my Heart. Stanly you dont drink.

STANLY. Madam, I am drinking draughts of Love from Cloe's eyes.

SOPHY. That's poor nourishment truly. Come, drink to her better acquaintance.

                     [MISS FITZGERALD *goes to a Closet & brings out a bottle*

MISS F. This, Ladies & Gentlemen is some of my dear Grandmother's own manufacture. She excelled in Gooseberry Wine. Pray taste it Lady Hampton?

LADY H. How refreshing it is!

MISS F. I should think with your Ladyship's permission, that Sir Arthur might taste a little of it.

LADY H. Not for Worlds. Sir Arthur never drinks any thing so high.

LORD F. And now my amiable Sophia condescend to marry me.

                     [He takes her hand & leads her to the front

STANLY. Oh! Cloe could I but hope you would make me blessed—

CLOE. I will.

                                 [They advance.

MISS F. Since you Willoughby are the only one left, I cannot refuse your earnest solicitations—There is my Hand.

LADY H. And may you all be Happy!

FINIS

The Mystery

An Unfinished Comedy

Dedication
To the Revd George Austen

SIR

     I humbly solicit your Patronage to the following Comedy, which tho' an unfinished one, is I flatter myself as *complete* a *Mystery* as any of its kind.

                         I am Sir your most Humle
                                    Servant
                                    THE AUTHOR

The Mystery

A Comedy

Dramatis Personae

MEN	WOMEN
Colonel Elliott	Fanny Elliott
Sir Edward Spangle	Mrs Humbug
Old Humbug	and
Young Humbug	Daphne
and	
Corydon	

Act the First

Scene the 1st
A Garden.

Enter CORYDON.

CORY.) But Hush! I am interrupted.

[*Exit* CORYDON

Enter OLD HUMBUG *& his* SON, *talking.*

OLD HUM:) It is for that reason I wish you to follow my advice. Are you convinced of its propriety?

YOUNG HUM:) I am Sir, and will certainly act in the manner you have pointed out to me.

OLD HUM:) Then let us return to the House.

[*Exeunt*

Scene the 2d

A Parlour in HUMBUG'S *House.*

MRS HUMBUG & FANNY, *discovered at work.*

MRS HUM:) You understand me my Love?

FANNY) Perfectly ma'am. Pray continue your narration.

MRS HUM:) Alas! it is nearly concluded, for I have nothing more to say on the Subject.

FANNY) Ah! here's Daphne.

Enter DAPHNE.

DAPHNE) My dear Mrs Humbug how d'ye do? Oh! Fanny t'is all over.

FANNY) Is it indeed!

MRS HUM:) I'm very sorry to hear it.

FANNY) Then t'was to no purpose that I. . . .

DAPHNE) None upon Earth.

MRS HUM:) And what is to become of? . . .

DAPHNE) Oh! thats all settled. (*whispers* MRS HUMBUG)

FANNY) And how is it determined?

DAPHNE) I'll tell you. (*whispers* FANNY)

MRS HUM:) And is he to? . . .

DAPHNE) I'll tell you all I know of the matter. (*whispers* MRS HUMBUG & FANNY)

FANNY) Well! now I know everything about it, I'll go [and dress][4] away.

MRS HUM: ⎫
          ⎬ And so will I.
DAPHNE ⎭

[Exeunt

Scene the 3d

 The Curtain rises and discovers SIR EDWARD SPANGLE *reclined in an elegant Attitude on a Sofa, fast asleep.*

Enter COLONEL ELLIOTT

COLONEL) My Daughter is not here I see . . . there lies Sir Edward . . . Shall I tell him the secret? . . . No, he'll certainly blab it. . . . But he is asleep and wont hear me. . . . So I'll e'en venture.

[Goes up to SIR EDWARD, whispers him, & Exit

End of the 1st *Act.*

_____

FINIS

_____

To Edward Austen Esqre

The following unfinished Novel
is respectfully inscribed
by
His obedient humle servt

THE AUTHOR

_____

[4] Erased in MS.

The Three Sisters

A Novel

Letter 1st

MISS STANHOPE TO MRS . . .

My dear Fanny

    I am the happiest creature in the World, for I have received an offer of marriage from Mr Watts. It is the first I have ever had & I hardly know how to value it enough. How I will triumph over the Duttons! I do not intend to accept it, at least I beleive not, but as I am not quite certain I gave him an equivocal answer & left him. And now my dear Fanny I want your Advice whether I should accept his offer or not, but that you may be able to judge of his merits & the situation of affairs I will give you an account of them. He is quite an old Man, about two & thirty, very plain *so* plain that I cannot bear to look at him. He is extremely disagreable & I hate him more than any body else in the world. He has a large fortune & will make great Settlements on me; but then he is very healthy. In short I do not know what to do. If I refuse him he as good as told me that he should offer himself to Sophia and if *she* refused him to Georgiana, & I could not bear to have either of them married before me. If I accept him I know I shall be miserable all the rest of my Life, for he is very ill tempered & peevish extremely jealous, & so stingy that there is no living in the house with him. He told me he should mention the affair to Mama, but I insisted upon it that he did not for very likely she would make me marry him whether I would or no; however probably he *has* before now, for he never does anything he is desired to do. I believe I shall have him. It will be such a triumph to be married before Sophy, Georgiana & the Duttons; And he promised to have a new Carriage on the occasion, but we almost quarrelled about the colour, for I insisted upon its being blue spotted with silver, & he declared it should be a plain Chocolate; & to provoke me more said it should be just as low as his old one. I wont have him I declare. He said he should come again tomorrow & take my final answer, so I believe I must get him while I can. I know the Duttons will envy me & I shall be able to chaprone Sophy & Georgiana to all the Winter Balls. But then what will be the use of that when very likely he wont let me go myself, for I know he hates dancing & [has a great idea of Womens never going from home][5] what he hates himself he has no idea of any other person's liking; & besides he talks a great deal of Women's always Staying at home & such stuff. I beleive I shant have him; I would refuse him at once if I were certain that neither of my Sisters would accept him, & that if they did not, he would not offer to the Duttons. I cannot run such a risk, so, if he will promise to have the Carriage ordered as I like, I will have him, if not he may ride in

---

[5] Erased in MS.

it by himself for me. I hope you like my determination; I can think of nothing better;
  And am your ever Affecte

MARY STANHOPE

FROM THE SAME TO THE SAME

DEAR FANNY

  I had but just sealed my last letter to you when my Mother came up & told me she
wanted to speak to me on a very particular subject.

  "Ah! I know what you mean; (said I) That old fool Mr Watts has told you all about it,
tho' I bid him not. However you shant force me to have him if I dont like it."

  "I am not going to force you Child, but only want to know what your resolution is
with regard to his Proposals, & to insist upon your making up your mind one way or
t'other, that if *you* dont accept him *Sophy* may."

  "Indeed (replied I hastily) Sophy need not trouble herself for I shall certainly marry
him myself."

  "If that is your resolution" (said my Mother) why should you be afraid of my forcing
your inclinations?"

  "Why, because I have not settled whether I shall have him or not."

  "You are the strangest Girl in the World Mary. What you say one moment, you unsay
the next. Do tell me once for all, whether you intend to marry Mr Watts or not?"

  "Law Mama how can I tell you what I dont know myself?"

  "Then I desire you will know, & quickly too, for Mr Watts says he wont be kept in
suspense."

  "That depends upon me."

  "No it does not, for if you do not give him your final answer tomorrow when he
drinks Tea with us, he intends to pay his Addresses to Sophy."

  "Then I shall tell all the World that he behaved very ill to me."

  "What good will that do? Mr Watts has been too long abused by all the World to
mind it now."

  "I wish I had a Father or a Brother because then they should fight him."

  "They would be cunning if they did, for Mr Watts would run away first; & therefore
you must & shall resolve either to accept or refuse him before tomorrow evening."

  "But why if I don't have him, must he offer to my Sisters?"

  "Why! because he wishes to be allied to the Family & because they are as pretty as
you are."

  "But will Sophy marry him Mama if he offers to her?"

  "Most likely. Why should not she? If however she does not choose it, then Georgiana
must, for I am determined not to let such an opportunity escape of settling one of my

Daughters so advantageously. So, make the most of your time; I leave you to settle the Matter with yourself." And then she went away. The only thing I can think of my dear Fanny is to ask Sophy & Georgiana whether they would have him were he to make proposals to them, & if they say they would not I am resolved to refuse him too, for I hate him more than you can imagine. As for the Duttons if he marries one of *them* I shall still have the triumph of having refused him first. So, adeiu my dear Freind—

YRS EVER M. S.

MISS GEORGIANA STANHOPE TO MISS X X X

MY DEAR ANNE   WEDNESDAY

Sophy & I have just been practising a little deceit on our eldest Sister, to which we are not perfectly reconciled, & yet the circumstances were such that if any thing will excuse it, they must. Our neighbour Mr Watts has made proposals to Mary; Proposals which she knew not how to receive, for tho' she has a particular Dislike to him (in which she is not singular) yet she would willingly marry him sooner than risk his offering to Sophy or me which in case of a refusal from herself, he told her he should do, for you must know the poor Girl considers our marrying before her as one of the greatest misfortunes that can possibly befall her, & to prevent it would willingly ensure herself everlasting Misery by a Marriage with Mr Watts. An hour ago she came to us to sound our inclinations respecting the affair which were to determine hers. A little before she came my Mother had given us an account of it, telling us that she certainly would not let him go farther than our own family for a Wife. "And therefore (said she) If Mary wont have him Sophy must, & if Sophy wont Georgiana *shall*." Poor Georgiana!—We neither of us attempted to alter my Mother's resolution, which I am sorry to say is generally more strictly kept than rationally formed. As soon as she was gone however I broke silence to assure Sophy that if Mary should refuse Mr Watts I should not expect her to sacrifice *her* happiness by becoming his Wife from a motive of Generosity to me, which I was afraid her Good nature & Sisterly affection might induce her to do.

"Let us flatter ourselves (replied She) that Mary will not refuse him. Yet how can I hope that my Sister may accept a Man who cannot make her happy."

"*He* cannot it is true but his Fortune, his Name, his House, his Carriage will and I have no doubt but that Mary will marry him; indeed why should she not? He is not more than two & thirty; a very proper age for a Man to marry at; He is rather plain to be sure, but then what is Beauty in a Man; if he has but a genteel figure & a sensible looking Face it is quite sufficient."

"This is all very true Georgiana but Mr Watts's figure is unfortunately extremely vulgar & his Countenance is very heavy."

"And then as to his temper; it has been reckoned bad, but may not the World be deceived in their Judgement of it. There is an open Frankness in his Disposition which becomes a Man; They say he is stingy; We'll call that Prudence. They say he is suspicious. *That* proceeds from a warmth of Heart always excusable in Youth, & in short I see no reason why he should not make a very good Husband, or why Mary should not be very happy with him."

Sophy laughed; I continued,

"However whether Mary accepts him or not I am resolved. My determination is made. I never would marry Mr Watts were Beggary the only alternative. So deficient in every respect! Hideous in his person and without one good Quality to make amends for it. His fortune to be sure is good. Yet not so very large! Three thousand a year. What is three thousand a year? It is but six times as much as my Mother's income. It will not tempt me."

"Yet it will be a noble fortune for Mary" said Sophy laughing again.

"For Mary! Yes indeed it will give me pleasure to see *her* in such affluence."

Thus I ran on to the great Entertainment of my Sister till Mary came into the room to appearance in great agitation. She sate down. We made room for her at the fire. She seemed at a loss how to begin & at last said in some confusion

"Pray Sophy have you any mind to be married?"

"To be married! None in the least. But why do you ask me? Are you acquainted with any one who means to make me proposals?"

"I—no, how should I? But may'nt I ask a common question?"

"Not a very *common* one Mary surely." (said I). She paused & after some moments silence went on—

"How should you like to marry Mr Watts Sophy?"

I winked at Sophy & replied for her. "Who is there but must rejoice to marry a man of three thousand a year. [who keeps a postchaise & pair, with silver Harness, a boot before & a window to look out at behind?"][6]

"Very true (she replied) That's very true. So you would have him if he would offer, Georgiana, & would *you* Sophy?"

Sophy did not like the idea of telling a lie & deceiving her Sister; she prevented the first & saved half her conscience by equivocation.

"I should certainly act just as Georgiana would do."

"Well then said Mary with triumph in her Eyes, *I* have had an offer from Mr Watts."

We were of course very much surprised; "Oh! do not accept him said I, and then perhaps he may have me."

In short my scheme took & Mary is resolved to do *that* to prevent our supposed happiness which she would not have done to ensure it in reality. Yet after all my Heart cannot acquit me & Sophy is even more scrupulous. Quiet our Minds my dear Anne by writing & telling us you approve our conduct. Consider it well over. Mary will have

---

[6] Erased in MS.

real pleasure in being a married Woman, & able to chaprone us, which she certainly shall do, for I think myself bound to contribute as much as possible to her happiness in a State I have made her choose. They will probably have a new Carriage, which will be paradise to her, & if we can prevail on Mr W. to set up his Phaeton she will be too happy. These things however would be no consolation to Sophy or me for domestic Misery. Remember all this & do not condemn us.

Friday.

Last night Mr Watts by appointment drank tea with us. As soon as his Carriage stopped at the Door, Mary went to the Window.

"Would you beleive it Sophy (said she) the old Fool wants to have his new Chaise just the colour of the old one, & hung as low too. But it shant—I *will* carry my point. And if he wont let it be as high as the Duttons, & blue spotted with Silver, I wont have him. Yes I will too. Here he comes. I know he'll be rude; I know he'll be illtempered & wont say one civil thing to me! nor behave at all like a Lover." She then sate down & Mr Watts entered.

"Ladies your most obedient." We paid our Compliments & he seated himself.

"Fine Weather Ladies." Then turning to Mary, "Well Miss Stanhope I hope you have *at last* settled the Matter in your own mind; & will be so good as to let me know whether you will *condescend* to marry me or not".

"I think Sir (said Mary) You might have asked in a genteeler way than that. I do not know whether I *shall* have you if you behave so odd."

"Mary!" (said my Mother) "Well Mama if he will be so cross. . . ."

"Hush, hush, Mary, you shall not be rude to Mr Watts."

"Pray Madam do not lay any restraint on Miss Stanhope by obliging her to be civil. If she does not choose to accept my hand, I can offer it else where, for as I am by no means guided by a particular preference to you above your Sisters it is equally the same to me which I marry of the three." Was there ever such a Wretch! Sophy reddened with anger & I felt *so* spiteful!

"Well then (said Mary in a peevish Accent) I *will* have you if I *must*."

"I should have thought Miss Stanhope that when such Settlements are offered as I have offered to you there can be no great violence done to the inclinations in accepting of them."

Mary mumbled out something, which I who sate close to her could just distinguish to be "What's the use of a great Jointure if Men live forever?" And then audibly "Remember the pinmoney; two hundred a year."

"A hundred and seventy-five Madam."

"Two hundred indeed Sir" said my Mother.

"And Remember I am to have a new Carriage hung as high as the Duttons', & blue

spotted with silver; and I shall expect a new saddle horse, a suit of fine lace, and an infi-
nite number of the most valuable Jewels. Diamonds such as never were seen, [Pearls as
large as those of the Princess Badroulbadour in the 4th Volume of the Arabian Nights
and Rubies, Emeralds, Toppazes, Sapphires, Amythists, Turkeystones, Agate, Beads,
Bugles & Garnets][7] and Pearls, Rubies, Emeralds and Beads out of number. You must
set up your Phaeton which must be cream coloured with a wreath of silver flowers
round it, You must buy 4 of the finest Bays in the Kingdom & you must drive me in it
every day. This is not all; You must entirely new furnish your House after my Taste, You
must hire two more Footmen to attend me, two Women to wait on me, must always let
me do just as I please & make a very good husband."

Here she stopped, I beleive rather out of breath.

"This is all very reasonable Mr Watts for my Daughter to expect."

"And it is very reasonable Mrs Stanhope that your daughter should be disappointed."
He was going on but Mary interrupted him "You must build me an elegant Greenhouse
& stock it with plants. You must let me spend every Winter in Bath, every Spring in
Town, Every Summer in taking some Tour, & every Autumn at a Watering Place, and
if we are at home the rest of the year (Sophy & I laughed) You must do nothing but
give Balls & Masquerades. You must build a room on purpose & a Theatre to act Plays
in. The first Play we have shall be *Which is the Man,* and I will do Lady Bell Bloomer."

"And pray Miss Stanhope (said Mr Watts) What am I to expect from you in return
for all this."

"Expect? why you may expect to have me pleased."

"It would be odd if I did not. Your expectations Madam are too high for me, & I must
apply to Miss Sophy who perhaps may not have raised her's so much."

"You are mistaken Sir in supposing so, (said Sophy) for tho' they may not be exactly
in the same Line, yet my expectations are to the full as high as my Sister's; for I expect
my Husband to be good tempered & Chearful; to consult my Happiness in all his
Actions, & to love me with Constancy & Sincerity."

Mr Watts stared. "These are very odd Ideas truly young Lady. You had better discard
them before you marry, or you will be obliged to do it afterwards."

My Mother in the meantime was lecturing Mary who was sensible that she had gone
too far, & when Mr Watts was just turning towards me in order I beleive to address me,
she spoke to him in a voice half humble, half sulky.

"You are mistaken Mr Watts if you think I was in earnest when I said I expected so
much. However I must have a new Chaise."

"Yes Sir, you must allow that Mary has a right to expect that."

"Mrs Stanhope, I *mean* & have always meant to have a new one on my Marriage. But
it shall be the colour of my present one."

"I think Mr Watts you should pay my Girl the compliment of consulting her Taste
on such Matters."

Mr Watts would not agree to this, & for some time insisted upon its being a Choco-

_____
[7] Erased in MS.

late colour, while Mary was as eager for having it blue with silver Spots. At length however Sophy proposed that to please Mr W. it should be a dark brown & to please Mary it should be hung rather high & have a silver Border. This was at length agreed to, tho' reluctantly on both sides, as each had intended to carry their point entire. We then proceeded to other Matters, & it was settled that they should be married as soon as the Writings could be completed. Mary was very eager for a Special Licence & Mr Watts talked of Banns A common Licence was at last agreed on. Mary is to have all the Family Jewels which are very inconsiderable I beleive & Mr W. promised to buy her a Saddle horse; but in return she is not to expect to go to Town or any other public place for these three Years. She is to have neither Greenhouse, Theatre or Phaeton; to be contented with one Maid without an additional Footman. It engrossed the whole Evening to settle these affairs; Mr W. supped with us & did not go till twelve. As soon as he was gone Mary exclaimed "Thank Heaven! he's off at last; how I do hate him!" It was in vain that Mama represented to her the impropriety she was guilty of in disliking him who was to be her Husband, for she persisted in declaring her aversion to him & hoping she might never see him again. What a Wedding will this be! Adeiu my dear Anne. Yr faithfully Sincere

Georgiana Stanhope

FROM THE SAME TO THE SAME

Dear Anne   Saturday

Mary eager to have every one know of her approaching Wedding & more particularly desirous of triumphing as she called it over the Duttons, desired us to walk with her this Morning to Stoneham. As we had nothing else to do we readily agreed, & had as pleasant a walk as we could have with Mary whose conversation entirely consisted in abusing the Man she is so soon to marry & in longing for a blue Chaise spotted with Silver. When we reached the Duttons we found the two Girls in the dressing-room with a very handsome Young Man, who was of course introduced to us. He is the son of Sir Henry Brudenell of Leicestershire—[Not related to the Family & even but distantly connected with it. His Sister is married to John Dutton's Wife's Brother. When you have puzzled over this account a little you will understand it.][8] Mr Brudenell is the handsomest Man I ever saw in my Life; we are all three very much pleased with him. Mary, who from the moment of our reaching the Dressing-room had been swelling with the knowledge of her own importance & with the Desire of making it known, could not remain long silent on the Subject after we were seated, & soon addressing herself to Kitty said,

"Dont you think it will be necessary to have all the Jewels new set?"

"Necessary for what?"

---

[8] Erased in MS.

"For What! Why for my appearance."

"I beg your pardon but I really do not understand you. What Jewels do you speak of, & where is your appearance to be made?"

"At the next Ball to be sure after I am married."

You may imagine their Surprise. They were at first incredulous, but on our joining in the Story they at last beleived it. "And who is it to" was of course the first Question. Mary pretended Bashfulness, & answered in Confusion her Eyes cast down "to Mr Watts". This also required Confirmation from us, for that anyone who had the Beauty & fortune (tho' small yet a provision) of Mary would willingly marry Mr Watts, could by them scarcely be credited. The subject being now fairly introduced and she found herself the object of every one's attention in company, she lost all her confusion & became perfectly unreserved & communicative.

"I wonder you should never have heard of it before for in general things of this Nature are very well known in the Neighbourhood."

"I assure you said Jemima I never had the least suspicion of such an affair. Has it been in agitation long?"

"Oh! Yes, ever since Wednesday."

They all smiled particularly Mr Brudenell.

"You must know Mr Watts is very much in love with me, so that it is quite a match of Affection on his side."

"Not on his only, I suppose" said Kitty.

"Oh! when there is so much Love on one side there is no occasion for it on the other. However I do not much dislike him tho' he is very plain to be sure."

Mr Brudenell stared, the Miss Duttons laughed & Sophy & I were heartily ashamed of our Sister. She went on.

"We are to have a new Postchaise & very likely may set up our Phaeton."

This we knew to be false but the poor Girl was pleased at the idea of persuading the company that such a thing was to be & I would not deprive her of so harmless an Enjoyment. She continued.

"Mr Watts is to present me with the family Jewels which I fancy are very considerable." I could not help whispering Sophy "I fancy not". "These Jewels are what I suppose must be new set before they can be worn. I shall not wear them till the first Ball I go to after my Marriage. If Mrs Dutton should not go to it, I hope you will let me chaprone you; I shall certainly take Sophy & Georgiana."

"You are very good (said Kitty) & since you are inclined to undertake the Care of young Ladies, I should advise you to prevail on Mrs Edgecumbe to let you chaprone her six Daughters which with your two Sisters and ourselves will make your Entrée very respectable."

Kitty made us all smile except Mary who did not understand her Meaning & coolly said that she should not like to chaprone so many. Sophy & I now endeavoured to change the conversation but succeeded only for a few Minutes, for Mary took care to bring back their attention to her & her approaching Wedding. I was sorry for my Sister's sake to see that Mr Brudenell seemed to take pleasure in listening to her account of it, & even encouraged her by his Questions & Remarks, for it was evident that his only Aim was to laugh at her. I am afraid he found her very ridiculous. He kept his Countenance extremely well, yet it was easy to see that it was with difficulty he kept it. At length however he seemed fatigued & Disgusted with her ridiculous Conversation, as he turned from her to us, & spoke but little to her for about half an hour before we left Stoneham. As soon as we were out of the House we all joined in praising the Person & Manners of Mr Brudenell.

We found Mr Watts at home.

"So, Miss Stanhope (said he) you see I am come a courting in a true Lover like Manner."

"Well you need not have *told* me that. I knew why you came very well."

Sophy & I then left the room, imagining of course that we must be in the way, if a Scene of Courtship were to begin. We were surprised at being followed almost immediately by Mary.

"And is your Courting so soon over?" said Sophy.

"Courting! (replied Mary) we have been quarrelling. Watts is such a Fool! I hope I shall never see him again."

"I am afraid you will, (said I) as he dines here to day. But what has been your dispute?"

"Why only because I told him that I had seen a Man much handsomer than he was this Morning, he flew into a great Passion & called me a Vixen, so I only stayed to tell him I thought him a Blackguard & came away."

"Short & sweet; (said Sophy) but pray Mary how will this be made up?"

"He ought to ask my pardon; but if he did, I would not forgive him."

"His Submission then would not be very useful."

When we were dressed we returned to the Parlour where Mama & Mr Watts were in close Conversation. It seems that he had been complaining to her of her Daughter's behaviour, & she had persuaded him to think no more of it. He therefore met Mary with all his accustomed Civility, & except one touch at the Phaeton & another at the Greenhouse, the Evening went off with great Harmony & Cordiality. Watts is going to Town to hasten the preparations for the Wedding.

I AM YOUR AFFECTE FREIND G.S.

To Miss Jane Anna Elizabeth Austen

MY DEAR NEICE

Though you are at this period not many degrees removed from Infancy, Yet trusting that you will in time be older, and that through the care of your excellent Parents, You will one day or another be able to read written hand, I dedicate to You the following Miscellanious Morsels, convinced that if you seriously attend to them, You will derive from them very important Instructions, with regard to your Conduct in Life.—If such my hopes should hereafter be realized, never shall I regret the Days and Nights that have been spent in composing these Treatises for your Benefit. I am my dear Neice

Your very Affectionate Aunt

THE AUTHOR

June 2d
1793

[A Fragment

written to inculcate the practise of Virtue

We all know that many are unfortunate in their progress through the world, but we do not know all that are so. To seek them out to study their wants, & to leave them unsupplied is the duty, and ought to be the Business of Man. But few have time, fewer still have inclination, and no one has either the one or the other for such employments. Who amidst those that perspire away their Evenings in crouded assemblies can have leisure to bestow a thought on such as sweat under the fatigue of their daily Labour.][9]

A BEAUTIFUL DESCRIPTION OF THE DIFFERENT EFFECTS OF SENSIBILITY ON DIFFERENT MINDS.

I am but just returned from Melissa's Bedside, & in my Life tho' it has been a pretty long one, & I have during the course of it been at many Bedsides, I never saw so affecting an object as she exhibits. She lies wrapped in a book muslin bedgown, a chambray gauze shift, and a french net nightcap. Sir William is constantly at her bedside. The only repose he takes is on the Sopha in

---

[9] Erased in MS.

the Drawing room, where for five minutes every fortnight he remains in an imperfect Slumber, starting up every Moment & exclaiming "Oh! Melissa, Ah! Melissa," then sinking down again, raises his left arm and scratches his head. Poor Mrs Burnaby is beyond measure afflicted. She sighs every now & then, that is about once a week; while the melancholy Charles says every Moment "Melissa how are you?" The lovely Sisters are much to be pitied. Julia is ever lamenting the situation of her friend, while lying behind her pillow & supporting her head—Maria more mild in her greif talks of going to Town next week, & Anna is always recurring to the pleasures we once enjoyed when Melissa was well.—I am usually at the fire cooking some little delicacy for the unhappy invalid—Perhaps hashing up the remains of an old Duck, toasting some cheese or making a Curry which are the favourite dishes of our poor friend.—In these situations we were this morning surprised by receiving a visit from Dr Dowkins; "I am come to see Melissa," said he. "How is She?" "Very weak indeed, said the fainting Melissa—"Very weak, replied the punning Doctor, aye indeed it is more than a very *week* since you have taken to your bed—How is your appetite?" "Bad, very bad, said Julia." "That *is* very bad—replied he. Are her spirits good, Madam?" "So poorly Sir that we are obliged to strengthen her with cordials every Minute."—"Well then she receives *Spirits* from your being with her. Does she sleep?" "Scarcely ever."—"And Ever Scarcely I suppose when she does. Poor thing! Does she think of dieing? "She has not strength to think at all. "Nay then she cannot think to have Strength."

The Generous Curate

a moral Tale, setting forth the
Advantages of being Generous and a Curate.

In a part little known of the County of Warwick, a very worthy Clergyman lately resided. The income of his living which amounted to about two hundred pound, & the interest of his Wife's fortune which was nothing at all, was entirely sufficient for the Wants & Wishes of a Family who neither wanted or wished for anything beyond what their income afforded them. Mr Williams had been in possession of his living above twenty Years, when this history commences, & his Marriage which had taken place soon after his presentation to it, had made him the father of six very fine Children. The eldest had been placed at the Royal Academy for Seamen at Portsmouth when about thirteen years old, and from thence had been discharged on board of one of the Vessels of a small fleet destined for Newfoundland, where his promising & amiable disposition had procured him many friends among the Natives, & from whence he regularly sent home a large Newfoundland Dog every Month to his family. The second, who was also a Son had been adopted by a neighbouring Clergyman with the intention of educating him at his own expence, which would have been a very desirable Circumstance had the Gentleman's fortune been equal to his generosity, but as he had nothing to support himself and a very large family but a Curacy of fifty pound a year, Young Williams knew nothing more at the age of 18 than what a twopenny Dame's School in the village could teach him. His Character however was perfectly amiable though his genius might be cramped, and he was addicted to no vice, or ever guilty of any fault beyond what his age and situation rendered perfectly excusable. He had indeed sometimes been detected in flinging Stones at a Duck or putting brickbats into his Benefactor's bed; but these innocent efforts of wit were considered by that good Man rather as the effects of a lively imagination, than of anything bad in his Nature, and if any punishment were decreed for the offence it was in general no greater than that the Culprit should pick up the Stones or take the brickbats away.—

FINIS

To Miss Austen, the following Ode to Pity is dedicated, from a thorough knowledge of her pitiful Nature, by her obedt humle Servt

THE AUTHOR

ODE TO PITY

1
Ever musing I delight to tread
  The Paths of honour and the Myrtle Grove
Whilst the pale Moon her beams doth shed
  On disappointed Love.
While Philomel on airy hawthorn Bush
  Sings sweet & Melancholy, And the thrush
Converses with the Dove.

2
Gently brawling down the turnpike road,
  Sweetly noisy falls the Silent Stream—
The Moon emerges from behind a Cloud
  And darts upon the Myrtle Grove her beam.
Ah! then what Lovely Scenes appear,
  The hut, the Cot, the Grot, & Chapel queer,
And eke the Abbey too a mouldering heap,
  Conceal'd by aged pines her head doth rear
And quite invisible doth take a peep.

END OF THE FIRST VOLUME

June 3d 1793